Fourth-Graders Don't Believe In Witches

**Look for these and
other Apple paperbacks
in your local bookstore!**

Cassie Bowen Takes Witch Lessons
by Anna Grossnickle Hines

The Ghostmobile
by Kathy Kennedy Tapp

The Secret Life of Dilly McBean
by Dorothy Haas

Ghosts Who Went to School
by Judith Spearing

The Witch Lady Mystery
by Carol Beach York

Fourth-Graders Don't Believe In Witches

Terri Fields

AN
APPLE
PAPERBACK

SCHOLASTIC INC.
New York Toronto London Auckland Sydney

ISBN 0-590-42804-7

12 11 10 9 8 7 6 5   2 3 4/9

Printed in the U.S.A.   28

First Scholastic printing, October 1989

Dedicated to Jeff Fields
who always believed
this book would come to be,
and with a special thanks to Lori

1

I should never have told my mother that I hated coming home to an empty house after school. I only said it because of Bobby Alexander. He'd tried almost the exact same words on his mom, and the next week she had quit her job and even volunteered to be his Cub Scout den leader.

I thought that sounded pretty nice. Besides, I didn't exactly love being a latchkey kid. I was always afraid I'd lose my key or something, and sometimes, I just wished I had someone to tell about my day. Since Mom hadn't been working for all that long, I figured she might not mind quitting if someone like me gave her a good reason why she should.

My plan seemed so simple that I still have trouble figuring out how it got so botched up. Things started off well enough. As soon as my mom got home from work, I put on my saddest-looking face and waited for her to ask me what was wrong. I had to hold that look for a long time, since she

1

took her time coming in and putting away her coat. But finally she sat down next to me and asked about my day. When she did, I looked extra upset and said, "I just hate being here all by myself every day after school. Maybe, if you quit work . . ."

At first, Mom got a very worried look on her face. "But Allan, I have to work . . ." She walked back and forth across the room, almost talking to herself. "I just can't be home, but maybe you really shouldn't be here all alone, especially if it's upsetting you."

Mom happened to glance out the window as she paced. Suddenly she exclaimed, "Why, that's it! Why didn't I think of it before! I'll bet that nice older lady who moved into the Millers' old house would be glad to take care of you!"

"But Mom," I protested. This was not the way things were supposed to be happening. "I don't want a baby-sitter." She didn't stop to listen; instead, she headed out the door and down the street. I watched her knock on the door of the old cottage two houses down. Oh, no, I thought as the door opened and my mother went inside.

She stayed there a long time. I kept my fingers crossed, hoping it was because the lady was explaining that she didn't want to baby-sit. After all, we didn't even know her; she'd only moved in a couple of weeks ago. I kept looking out the window, wishing Mom would hurry home and make it official that I was still on my own. I mean, I didn't want some old lady taking care of me; I wanted my mom home.

Finally Mom walked back into our house. "Well, that's settled," she said with a pleased grin on her face. "Actually I haven't been very happy about your being home alone, either." She went into the kitchen to start dinner, and I followed her explaining that I really didn't need some old-lady baby-sitter at our house. "Oh, Allan. She's not some old-lady baby-sitter. Her name is Mrs. Mullins, and she seems quite nice. You'll like her. She prefers that you go to her house, which should be a rather fun adventure, don't you think?"

I didn't think it would be a fun adventure at all; in fact, I was sure I would hate it, but Mom didn't wait for my answer. She just added, "Mrs. Mullins will be expecting you every day after school starting tomorrow, and you can stay there until I get home."

Mom was so pleased that she began to hum while she made dinner, but I groaned loudly. There were lots of latchkey kids in my class, and none of them had baby-sitters. When everyone found out about my baby-sitter, the kids would tease me forever. I wasn't exactly Mr. Popularity now, and I sure didn't need it going around the school that I was a baby. With that awful thought in mind, I even gave up my favorite TV program to spend every minute I could until bedtime trying to talk my mother out of this baby-sitter idea. "I was only kidding about being lonely," I said. I begged, I argued, I even told her that if I were home alone, I would clean up the house after school. Mom wouldn't listen. She thought the whole idea of my going to Mrs. Mullins's was terrific, and nothing I said was making any difference at all. That is why I, Allan Hobart, was probably going to be the only kid in the entire fourth grade who was stuck with a baby-sitter. I was mortified.

The next afternoon I walked home from school as slowly as possible, trying to get to Mrs. Mullins's as late as I could. That way I wouldn't have to talk much to her. I knew all about old ladies from the time I'd visited my great-aunt in Maine. They pinched your cheeks, they treated you as if you were two years old, and you had to shout to make them hear anything you said.

Facing all that every day was more than any nine-year-old boy should have to handle. Somehow, I was going to get out of this mess, but about the only way I could think of was to be so terrible that Mrs. Mullins would tell my mother she didn't want me there anymore. I would probably get in a lot of trouble, but it would be better than this.

Stupid Bobby Alexander and his dumb ideas! I thought as I turned up the walkway to Mrs. Mullins's front door. It wasn't fair that his mom was home helping him work on Wolf Pack badges while I was stuck with some awful old lady. Even her house was old. The green paint was peeling off the front door, and the white house showed patches of brown. It had been empty forever. Though we'd never actually done it, my friends and I had talked about trying to sneak in and use it for a clubhouse. Actually it was Jeff, Jason, and Bobby who talked about sneaking in. I was just sort of hanging around them.

Anyway, I never found out whether I could actually go with them or not because before they set a time to sneak in, the For Sale sign went down. I'd crossed my fingers and hoped a family with a nice kid my age would move in. I figured I could get to know him before he knew anyone else, and we might be best friends. Instead, some old lady with no kids at all moved in. Pounding my toe into the sidewalk, I sighed. Then I dragged my feet up the front walk and pushed the doorbell. Mrs. Mullins was probably going to gush about what a cute little boy I was. Ugh! She might even want to read me some fairy tales! I was *not* listening to any fairy tales! Suddenly I realized that no one had answered the door. Maybe she's not here, I hoped. I rang the bell again. If no one answered this time, I could go home, and my mom would be mad at the old lady instead of me. I smiled at the thought.

Just then the door opened. I gulped. It was just as I had suspected. The lady standing there even looked like my great-aunt in Maine. I tried to prepare my cheeks to be pinched, but surprisingly, Mrs. Mullins didn't reach for them. "Oh, it's you," she said sounding annoyed. "Well, I guess you should come in. What's your name again?"

This reception wasn't exactly the gushing excitement I thought it would be, but that was fine. It would probably just make my plan work more easily, and Mrs. Mullins would be glad to get rid of me. Scowling, I shouted loudly to make sure she heard, "My name's Allan, Allan Hobart."

"Well, there's no need to shout about it, and there's certainly no point to standing here letting bugs in. You may enter; shut the door behind you, please."

I scowled even harder in case Mrs. Mullins didn't see too well, because she hadn't mentioned that I looked unhappy. Just in case she wasn't going to notice at all, I said, "I really don't want to be here!"

Mrs. Mullins looked at me and returned my scowl. "Well, that's fine, because I really don't want you to be here, either."

"You don't?" I said, beginning to get confused. "But my mom —"

"Your mother seems very nice, but she certainly is determined. Oh, I tried, I really did. But I couldn't talk her out of the idea that your coming here after school was a wonderful idea. Besides, mothers always get so upset if I try to explain about . . ." Mrs. Mullins's penetrating green eyes grew large and she clamped her mouth firmly shut as if she'd said too much already.

"Explain about what?" I asked.

Mrs. Mullins stared at me the same way my math teacher did when she wasn't sure I'd done my homework. "Never you mind," she sniffed.

There was something about the way she said it that made me sure I wanted to know what it was. "Gee, I won't tell anyone else, really I won't."

"Tell what?" she asked.

"What you started to tell me."

Mrs. Mullins fixed her green eyes on me. "I don't remember starting to tell you anything at all." And with that she turned and walked out of the room.

I stood in the entryway totally confused. This was just great; why did these things always happen to me? Not only was I going to be the laughingstock of the fourth grade for having a babysitter, but I had to have the crabbiest one in the whole world. "What a witch!" I said aloud, kicking my foot against the carpet.

With that Mrs. Mullins came bursting back into the room. She put her hands on her hips. "What did you just say?" she demanded.

"Uh, nothing."

Her voice got real high and she said, "Oh, yes, you did. I heard you! What did you say?"

If she heard me, I didn't know why she needed me to repeat it. I did know that if she told my mom, I'd be in big trouble. I could hear my mom now: "You called that sweet, little lady a witch? Allan Hobart, I'm ashamed . . . ."

Maybe Mrs. Mullins hadn't heard exactly what I'd said. Then again, maybe she had, and if I lied, I'd get in trouble for being rude *and* for lying. It was definitely a no-win situation, so I just didn't say anything.

Mrs. Mullins tapped her foot. "Did you call me a witch?" So she had heard, after all.

I bit my lip, "Well, yeah, but I didn't mean to. What I mean is that . . . uh . . . of course, you're not a witch." I could feel my face getting red.

Mrs. Mullins took a step toward me. "I take it you don't like witches."

8

This had to be the weirdest lady I'd ever met. How could my mother have done this to me! Mrs. Mullins was waiting for me to say something. "Uh, no, why would anyone like a witch? They're ugly."

"Oh, really?" She seemed interested.

"Yeah, real ugly. And they do terrible things." I was getting warmed up now, and I let my imagination go. It was better than standing in all that silence. "They take bats' wings, and dried-up blood, and old toads, and lots of other gross stuff, and they wait until midnight, and then they make awful spells."

Mrs. Mullins bit her lip, and I thought maybe I'd scared her, which made me feel real bad. "Listen, it's okay, though. You don't have to worry or be scared or anything, because the good news is that there *are* no real witches."

"You know that for certain, do you?"

"Oh, yeah, I'm absolutely sure!" I replied, feeling pretty important. Imagine, me knowing more than an old lady like her. "So you don't have to worry about any dumb witches at all. They can't hurt you because they're just make-believe."

The corners of Mrs. Mullins's mouth began to turn upward, and her eyes started to twinkle. "I see," she replied. Suddenly my blue Cubs baseball cap sailed off my head and began to fly around the room faster and faster. My eyes were getting dizzy following it. Then my hat dropped *kerplop!* at my feet.

"Wow! Did you just see that?" I shouted. "How did that happen?"

Mrs. Mullins didn't say a word. She just turned on her heel and marched out of the room.

2

I bent over to retrieve my cap and stared at it very carefully. It was definitely the same Cubs cap that had been on my head only a minute ago. "Hats don't fly," I said to an empty room; yet that was exactly what this hat had just done.

Okay, so it did fly, but there's got to be a reason, I told myself, holding on to it tightly. I thought it over. It's got to be some kind of a trick. I squinted my eyes to see if there was some sort of string on the ceiling, but nothing was there. This was some trick!

Then I thought about Jeff Wilson. He was the most popular kid in the fourth grade; the captain of every team, while I was just the "yeah, I'll take him" kid who never got picked first or last — a nobody to fill up the middle. But suppose, I thought to myself, suppose I could walk in and make everyone's hat fly off his or her head. Then they'd notice! I grinned. This Mrs. Mullins definitely needed more investigation. Anxious to unravel her tricks, I marched into the kitchen.

Mrs. Mullins was sitting at the kitchen table. She had her hand on her chin and her forehead was wrinkled in thought. I waited a minute, not wanting to interrupt her, but it didn't seem as if she was ever going to stop muttering and look at me. "Um, excuse me," I said, "but that was a pretty neat trick, I mean with my cap. How did you do it, anyway?"

Mrs. Mullins looked confused. "Trick . . . that wasn't a trick. Look, Allan, I really think it was a mistake for me to say I'd baby-sit. It just isn't going to work out."

"Yes, it will, Mrs. Mullins. Listen, you don't even have to baby-sit me all year or anything. Just teach me how to make hats fly off people's heads."

"I will do no such thing!" She stared at me. "Now, please, just go into the other room and leave me alone."

I'd been totally dismissed. Mrs. Mullins wasn't going to reveal anything, so I walked into what looked like a normal little-old-lady living room and sat down on a blue-flowered sofa. This afternoon sure hadn't been anything like what I'd thought it would be. I decided I'd start looking for the string or wire that must have pulled my cap off my head. First, I walked around the room very slowly, waving my hands in front of me so I'd feel

12

the string. When I found nothing, I crawled around on the floor trying to find a clue to her trick.

Mrs. Mullins entered the room just as I was lying on my stomach reaching under the sofa. "What are you doing?" she asked. "Are you stuck?"

I jumped up. "I'm fine," I said.

"Oh?" she replied. "Most people sit *on* sofas, not *under* them!" Her green eyes stared at me. I grew more uncomfortable by the minute. Maybe I'd better try talking about something else besides my hat. If I led up to it slowly, maybe she'd tell me how it had flown.

"So, uh, have you been a baby-sitter" (how I hated that word!) "for a lot of kids?"

Mrs. Mullins pushed her wire-rimmed glasses up on her nose. "Not really. Actually you're my first one. And you don't look much like a baby."

I was glad she'd at least noticed. Though I didn't mean to say anything, I blurted out, "You know, you're pretty weird. I mean, haven't all old ladies done lots of baby-sitting?"

She began to tap her foot quickly against the carpet as she folded her arms against her chest. "Well, I've had many other important things to do. I guess I should have been firmer with your mother. I really have no idea what to do with a nine-year-old boy."

13

This was my opportunity to get out of having Mrs. Mullins as my baby-sitter. I was pretty sure I could get Mrs. Mullins to tell my mom that she didn't want to baby-sit me, but I had a strange feeling I'd be sorry if I did. Mrs. Mullins wasn't like any person I'd ever met. For one thing, old ladies were supposed to think kids like me were just adorable; this one thought I was nothing but a pain in the neck. For another thing, even if I managed to ditch Mrs. Mullins, my mom would only find another baby-sitter, and at least I might eventually convince this one to teach me her trick. "Mrs. Mullins—" I started to ask, but she interrupted me.

"Allan, please, just stop asking me questions." That was the last thing she said to me all afternoon. That didn't discourage me, because I knew that when adults absolutely didn't want you to ask questions, those were the questions with the most interesting answers. And so I, Allan Hobart, the kid who'd made up his mind to get rid of this baby-sitter today, had now decided that I'd be back tomorrow for sure.

When I got home, Mom asked me about Mrs. Mullins, and I didn't say too much except that I guessed I'd try it for another day or two. Mom smiled. "I know you're going to like her. Tell me all about your afternoon." Just then the telephone rang. By the time my mom had gotten off an hour

14

later, she had forgotten I'd never answered her question. I didn't remind her, because I wasn't sure what to say.

I felt pretty good as I got dressed for the next day at school. Not only was I going to find out more about weird old Mrs. Mullins after school, but it was time for Miss Jenkins to choose a new Media Monitor. Since I was the only one who still hadn't had a turn, today had to be my chance!

All through the Pledge of Allegiance, I worried that Miss Jenkins might forget today was the day, but she didn't. Right after morning announcements she said, "It's time to name our new Media Monitor." I sat up a little straighter. It was going to be fun to be in charge of all the video equipment for the week.

Miss Jenkins looked at her sheet of paper. "I believe that everyone who signed up has had a chance, and so today, we'll start giving second chances. Steve . . . ."

It took all my courage, but I raised my hand. "Miss Jenkins, I still haven't had a first chance."

Miss Jenkins checked her list again. "Oh, I seem to have forgotten you. I'm sorry, Allan."

Jennifer called out, "That's okay, Miss Jenkins; he's just a forgettable kind of guy."

The class laughed, and I tried to laugh with them like it was no big deal. Miss Jenkins looked at Jennifer. "That wasn't necessary, Jennifer. It was my error, and Allan will be our new Media Monitor."

I sighed. I'd been waiting ever since school started for it to be my turn, and now it was sort of spoiled. Unfortunately Jennifer was right. I wasn't the most hated kid; that was Billy Pickins. I wasn't the most picked on one; that was Emily Chance, but I was sure I was the most forgettable. Sometimes, I felt practically invisible. Feeling sorry for myself, I tugged at my baseball cap, and suddenly I started to smile. As soon as I learned Mrs. Mullins's trick, I wouldn't ever be the invisible kid again.

Finally school was out, and I ran toward Mrs. Mullins's house. It wasn't until I went to ring the front doorbell that I stopped to remember that Mrs. Mullins and I weren't exactly best buddies, and she might not be thrilled to see me again.

I waited on the doorstep for what seemed like forever before the door opened. Mrs. Mullins looked surprised. "Oh, my goodness, is it time for you to be back?"

"Boy, it would sure be nice if everyone didn't keep forgetting about me!" That wasn't the greeting I'd intended. It just sort of popped out.

"Oh, I don't know," Mrs. Mullins replied, letting me into the house. "It's not always so great to be well-known, either. I . . . uh . . . I didn't expect you for awhile. Why don't you just have a seat in the living room."

At that moment, there was a big popping sound, and a gigantic blob of green rolled out of the kitchen. "Yikes!" I shouted. "Run, Mrs. Mullins; there's a monster in your house!"

"Allan, don't shout; it's okay. Really, it is. That's just green jelly."

The quivering blob had stopped a few inches in front of me. I could smell the mint, but I'd never seen anything like this. Even if they dumped the whole grocery store of jellies out on the floor, it wouldn't make this big of a blob. I took a couple of steps backward. My knees felt sort of wobbly. "Uh, Mrs. Mullins," I said hoarsely, "what's it doing here?"

Mrs. Mullins looked all flustered. "I . . . uh . . . I'd started a . . . I'd started something before you came, and when I answered the door, I guess it kept on working . . . or . . . maybe. . . . Oh, I don't know."

I knew *I* didn't know. "What are we going to do with it?" I asked, my eyes never leaving the quivering, shimmering green mass.

Mrs. Mullins seemed to snap back to attention. "That's right. We'd better get rid of it before someone else sees it. We'll . . . uh . . . we'll put

17

it on the lawn in the backyard. Let's see . . . I have some shovels in the garage. Would you get them?"

I walked into the garage pinching myself to make sure I was awake, and this whole situation was real. When I returned with the shovels, I half expected to find both Mrs. Mullins and the green mess gone, but they both were there waiting.

"Mrs. Mullins, I just don't understand. How did this green blob happen?" I started to ask more questions, but she cut me off.

"Not now. We've got to get rid of this stuff. Then we can talk." So, for the next hour, Mrs. Mullins and I scooped shovelfuls of green jelly into buckets and dumped them on the back lawn, which started getting kind of sticky. I suggested that maybe we should try the front lawn, but Mrs. Mullins said, "Absolutely not! No one must know about this."

While I shoveled, I began to wonder if instead of a magician, Mrs. Mullins was some kind of nutty scientist. Pretty soon my hands and my back started to hurt from carrying all that goop, but I had to admit, the day had been a lot more interesting than it would have been sitting at home.

Finally we got all of the green goop outside. It sort of melted into the lawn, and there was a nice mint smell throughout the whole backyard. We finished the last shovelful and flopped down on the living room chairs.

"Mrs. Mullins, now . . ." I said. "I've worked for the last hour, and I haven't said a word, but now you've got to tell me what's going on. Yesterday, my hat. Today, the green blob."

Mrs. Mullins tapped her finger against the table. "Why don't we just forget about both those little items."

"Are you kidding me?" My voice rose in anger. "Mrs. Mullins, I've just practically killed myself shoveling out the biggest blob of green jelly in the world, and now, you want me to forget about it? You said we could talk after we got rid of it. I wish I could have taken pictures of the blob to show the kids at school!"

Mrs. Mullins looked horrified. "You mustn't even think of doing such a thing." She took a deep breath. Half to herself, she said, "I know this is a mistake, but I don't see any way around it." Then she glared at me. "Allan Hobart, can you keep a secret?"

"Of course, I can!" I replied.

"Very well, this is my secret, and Allan, it's the most important thing in the world to me that *no one* ever finds it out. Do you understand?"

"Yes, ma'am!" I had to admit that I was excited. Maybe she was a world-famous magician who was in disguise from her fans. Maybe. . . .

Mrs. Mullins straightened her gold-rimmed glasses and cleared her throat as if she had a very important announcement to make. Then she hesitated. "I think I'd better find out a little more about you before I decide for certain what to do. Just who is Allan Hobart?"

"Well, I . . . I'm me. I'm the kid who lives down the street. I'm the kid that you're baby-sitting. You know who I am!"

"That won't do at all," she replied.

"Okay." I thought a minute. "Well, I'm nine, and I'm in fourth grade at Miller Elementary School."

"And . . . ?" she continued questioning.

"And I don't know. People don't ask questions like this!"

"I do," she replied. "Well, I'm waiting. . . ."

I took a deep breath and blurted out, "My name is Allan Hobart. My favorite thing at school is recess. Math isn't too bad, either. When I grow up, I want to be a professional baseball player. I live with my mom. She works; she doesn't want me to stay home alone. That's why I'm here. She didn't use to work. I used to live with both my parents, but they got divorced, and my dad moved away. It's really no big deal, though. Lots of kids have parents who split up." I said the whole thing without even taking a breath, and it was all the truth except for two parts. First, though I really wanted to be a professional baseball player some day, I knew I'd never make it unless I got a whole lot better. Second, it was a real big deal about my parents' divorce. At night in bed, I cried about it for a long, long time, but I certainly wasn't going to tell Mrs. Mullins about that. "Well, that's it," I said. "That's all there is to know about me. Now, what's your secret?"

Mrs. Mullins didn't answer directly. "Allan, are you scared of witches?"

I couldn't see where this was leading us. I figured it was just more conversation to keep me from ever finding out Mrs. Mullins's secret.

"Of course I'm not," I said. "I told you yesterday that witches are just pretend."

Mrs. Mullins seemed to ignore me. "You have no idea how many people are frightened of witches." I noticed that she was so short her feet didn't completely touch the floor as she sat on the sofa. "That's why I vowed that when I moved here, no one would ever know. Then I lost my temper yesterday because of your rude remarks about witches, and without stopping to think, I made your hat fly. That might have been okay, if I just hadn't had that jelly spell go wrong after you'd come in the door. It was supposd to make a quart of raspberry jam. I don't know quite why it made twenty-five gallons of mint jelly." Mrs.

Mullins sighed again. "Do you understand? Remember, you've promised never to tell anyone my secret."

I didn't quite understand anything, and I said so.

Mrs. Mullins hopped off the sofa and stood proudly. Her eyes glowed green as she solemnly announced, "Allan Hobart, I am a witch."

3

I kept hearing Mrs. Mullins's words in my head the whole way home, but I couldn't quite believe them. The phone was ringing as I got in the door, and I half expected it would be Mrs. Mullins, saying it was all just a joke. I picked up the phone, and Mom's voice came out. "Honey, I'm at this meeting, and I can't get out of it. Have some cold cuts for dinner, do your homework, and I'll be home as soon as I can." I told her I would. "Allan, you sound strange; is everything okay?" she asked.

"Sure, Mom, I'm fine. I was just thinking, I guess." I hung up the phone. Actually I had never thought so hard. I knew that there was no such thing as a witch, but it explained how Mrs. Mullins could have made my hat fly. It was a good reason why a huge blob of green jelly could roll out of the kitchen. And then there was the look in Mrs. Mullins's eyes when she told me. She didn't look like she was teasing at all. She looked real proud,

23

and yet she looked real sad. It all just didn't make sense.

The next day at school, I went to the library and asked the librarian where I could find books on witches. "Gee," she replied. "Halloween isn't for awhile, but all the books on witches would be in the fiction section."

"Uh . . . isn't fiction the stuff that isn't true?" I asked.

"Why, that's right, young man. That's very good. I can never keep all you kids straight — what's your name again?"

"It's Allan," I replied, but my thoughts weren't on school. I walked over to the Halloween books. The witches in them wore pointed black hats and were tall and skinny with long noses. Mrs. Mullins looked nothing like that.

All right, I told myself. Witches are not real. Mrs. Mullins is definitely real. Yet Mrs. Mullins is a witch. Somehow, it just didn't add up.

That afternoon when I got to Mrs. Mullins's house, she greeted me uncertainly. "Did you tell anyone my secret today?"

"Of course not," I replied. "Mrs. Mullins, I never, ever break my promises. Really, you can trust me for sure, but can I ask you a question?"

Mrs. Mullins leaned her elbows on the table and put her hands under her chin. "You certainly ask a lot of questions."

"Well, I've never met a witch before, and you're the only person I can talk to about it. So tell me, is there something special about this house that makes it good for a witch? Is that why you moved here?" I was thinking to myself that witches were supposed to live in caves.

Mrs. Mullins sighed. "No, there's nothing special about this house at all."

"Then why did you move here?"

Mrs. Mullins seemed deep in thought. I wondered if she even remembered that I was still there. "I really loved my old house. I loved the way the bedroom window caught the morning sunlight, and I loved walking down the tree-lined street in front of my house. I just didn't deserve to have the neighborhood folks kick me out."

"Wow! What kind of people throw out a little old lady from their neighborhood?"

Mrs. Mullins looked at me as if she were startled I was still there. "Ones who think that that little old lady is a witch." She smoothed her skirt, and I could swear that I saw tears in her eyes.

"What did you do to them to make them kick you out?" I wondered if I were in danger.

"Do to them? Why, I only invited them to what was supposed to be a wonderful party. They had asked me to so many garden teas and dinner parties. Finally I invited them to come and watch a spell. Oh, it was a wonderful spell." Her voice got excited. "There was this big poof of pink smoke, and then my whole little house looked like a castle. There was a band playing music, all kinds of food."

"Wow, what a surprise! Didn't they love it?"

Mrs. Mullins ran her hand through her hair. "That's what I'd hoped. It was to be such a lovely party. But everyone left before the party could really begin."

"Wow!" I said again, trying to imagine a regular old house looking like a castle. "Then what happened?"

"Well, I waited until the spell wore off and my house looked normal again, and then I tried to go talk to my neighbors. I tried to explain that some folks like to garden; I like to perform spells. I would never hurt anyone with my spells any more than they'd hurt anyone with their flowers." Mrs. Mullins's lip trembled. "But they wouldn't listen. We'd been neighbors for years, and I'd always gotten along with everyone just fine. That's why I figured it wouldn't matter if I shared some spells with them. But suddenly everything changed. Children began throwing eggs at my house. No one would talk to me. Finally I had to move."

"Gee, I'm really sorry."

She glared at me. "I don't need anyone to be sorry for me. I'm just fine. However, I don't want to move again, Allan Hobart, and that is why I do not want anyone here to find out I am a witch.

26

I intend to blend in perfectly . . . no one will remember or care who I am."

"You're not going to like that, Mrs. Mullins. Really, you won't."

"Oh, and what makes you so sure?"

I shrugged. "I'm just sure, that's all."

"Well," said Mrs. Mullins, "I'm ready to try it. Now, I think that we should forget that I am a witch and you are a very nosy nine-year-old boy. Just what is it that baby-sitters" (Mrs. Mullins said the word with almost as much disgust as I felt for it) "and little kids do together?"

I didn't answer because I didn't want to talk about baby-sitters. I'd had them all my life, and they were boring. I wanted to talk about witches. Fourth-graders didn't believe in witches, and yet I didn't know how else to explain Mrs. Mullins.

"When did you do your first spell?" I asked.

Mrs. Mullins sighed in disgust. "I can see that we'd better just get this over with or you'll keep asking questions forever. I'll answer them today, and then that's it. I started doing spells when my mother gave me my recipe book."

"A *recipe* book?" I interrupted.

Mrs. Mullins shook her head in amazement. "I suppose you didn't know that witches had recipe books. What do they teach you children in school?"

I scratched my head. "Well, I —"

Mrs. Mullins interrupted. "Never mind." She

pushed her glasses back up on her nose and sighed. "I kept every one of my thousands of spells in a big brown book marked *RECIPES* on the cover. When I moved, I waited to pack it until the very last minute. I put it on the very top of the final box the moving men took; I know I did. But when I got here and unpacked . . ." Mrs. Mullins spread her hands to show they were empty. "The book was gone."

"Well, did you look for it?" I asked. "If you're sure you packed it, it's got to be here."

"Of course, I looked for my book! What a silly question! I've gone over every nook and cranny of this whole house. I called the movers to see if the book fell off the truck. I called the people who bought my old house. No, my magic book, filled with all the years of spells I've done, is just missing!"

I really didn't know what to say. I tried to think how I'd feel if I lost my lucky yellow rabbit's foot. I knew I'd feel really terrible, and my rabbit's foot couldn't even do anything magic like Mrs. Mullins's book. "Well, at least you probably knew most of the spells," I said, trying to make her feel better. "I mean, since you're old, you've probably done them all lots of times, right?"

Mrs. Mullins frowned. "I'm not *that* old. Besides, there were thousands of spells in that book. Come with me, young man." She led me into the kitchen, stood on her tiptoes, and opened the three cabinets next to the sink. They were filled with jars. There were hundreds and hundreds of them, and each jar looked exactly the same as the last except that the names were different. Mrs. Mullins pulled one from the shelf and held it up to me. "A little more white essence of tecolet, and good heavens! there'd be totally different results." Mrs. Mullins shook her head sadly. Obviously she expected me to understand what white essence of tecolet was all about, so I didn't say anything.

She put the jar back, closed the cabinet, and sat down at the kitchen table. "So you can see that without my spell book, nothing works right. Like yesterday. Your hat was supposed to turn into a bird, a yellow canary, I think."

"Gee . . . I'm sorry," I said. "Maybe you should try it again." I crossed my fingers and hoped.

"Oh, it wouldn't work right. Nothing has. When I first moved into this house, I missed my old shade tree. No problem, I thought. I'll just create one in the backyard of this house. I got my ingredients, dumped them on the ground, and chanted my chant. And instead of a tree, I got a big toad who croaked twice and hopped away."

I sneaked a look out the window into Mrs. Mullins's backyard. There was definitely no tree there. Of course, that didn't prove anything. There never had been a tree there, and Mrs. Mullins may have just noticed a frog instead of actually producing one. On the other hand, suppose she really had created a toad out of nothing. Wasn't that as incredible as if she'd created a tree? I just wasn't sure what to think.

A clock on the wall began to chime. Mrs. Mullins and I listened to the chimes finish. "Allan, it's six, and your mother wants you to walk home at six. You'd best be going." Mrs. Mullins's voice sounded so normal. It didn't seem possible that we'd just been talking of trees turning into toads and missing magic books.

I didn't want to go home. Yeah, I know. I hadn't wanted to come here, either, but that was before I'd met Mrs. Mullins. She was weird, but she certainly was not boring. Besides, I wanted to find her magic book, that is, if there really was such a book. Mrs. Mullins, however, had already stood up and walked toward the door. I got the hint. "Well, uh, I'll see you tomorrow," I said standing up. I added, "Maybe tomorrow I could help you look for the book again or something, okay?"

Mrs. Mullins didn't say anything, so I went home. My mom was already there when I got in the door. "Honey, I'm so sorry that we haven't had a chance to really talk for the past two days. Tonight there'll be no telephone calls and no meetings. All day, I've been wondering about you and Mrs. Mullins. Now, I want to know exactly how the two of you are getting along. I must confess that when I met her, she reminded me exactly of a baby-sitter I used to have when I was young."

I almost blurted out, "You mean you had a witch for a baby-sitter, too?" but I caught myself in time. A promise was a promise. "Uh, she's okay," I said. "I guess it'll be okay to go back."

"Oh, good," my mother said. "You'll see that it's much better than coming home to an empty house. I think she's going to be just perfect for you."

I bit my lip to keep from laughing. Perfect to my mother, I was sure, was not a little old lady who didn't like kids, had never baby-sat before, and thought she was a witch, but it might, in fact, be just perfect for me!

4

The next day school was going along in its own boring way when Jennifer started writing a note to Karen. Now, Mrs. Jenkins had a firm rule in our class. No note writing. If you got caught, you had to read your note to the whole class, plus you had to stay after school and write an apology to the teacher. I happened to have the wonderful luck of sitting between Jennifer and Karen, and guess on whose desk the note landed when they passed it. It wasn't even folded shut, I guess, because Jennifer thought it wouldn't look like a note that way. I picked it up to pass it on, and since it was open, I just sort of read it for a minute. The note said, *Super cute boys: Jason, Jeff, Bobby, Andy, Jim. Cute boys: Kevin, Steve, Marc. Ugly boys: Gary, Johnny, Ryan. Super ugly boys: Billy. Do you agree? Write back.* My name, I noticed, hadn't been mentioned at all. I was thinking that it was probably better not to be mentioned at all than to be one of the "uggers" when I looked up and saw Miss Jenkins standing next to my desk.

"I'll take the note, Allan."

"But . . ."

She took the note from my hands and read it to herself. "I'm not going to read this note aloud because I think it would be unfair to some students," said Miss Jenkins, "but I'll see you after school, Allan."

"Hey, I didn't write it!"

Miss Jenkins scowled. "Boys and girls, when we covered the class rules, I told you that I wasn't going to waste valuable class time trying to track down who wrote unsigned notes. I said that I'd simply give detention to whomever was reading the note. Allan, I'm afraid, in this case, that is you."

The day dragged on. Finally the dismissal bell rang. Everyone else filed out while I, Allan Hobart, sat in my seat. " 'Bye, Allan," Jennifer called from the doorway, just to emphasize the point.

How did Jennifer always get away with stuff like that? Just once I'd like to get even with her!

I was almost a half hour late by the time I got to Mrs. Mullins's, and I was feeling good and sorry for myself. Probably Mrs. Mullins was glad I was late. It gave her more time not to be bothered with a nosy nine-year-old kid. I punched at the doorbell, and to my surprise, the door opened immediately.

"Aren't you a little late today?" Mrs. Mullins's white hair was swept into a bun, and she was wearing a red shapeless sweater. Her hand was in one pocket, and for a minute, I almost thought she was going to pull something magic out of it, but all that came out of the pocket was her hand.

"I had to stay after school," I mumbled.

"Ahh, does that happen often?" she asked.

"No." I didn't feel like going over the whole thing again, and Mrs. Mullins didn't ask.

"I thought maybe you'd decided you didn't want to be around a witch." Mrs. Mullins looked a little unsure of herself. I guess I recognized the look because I'd felt that way lots of times myself.

"Hey, I'm ready to look for your recipe book," I said. "Let's get going."

We divided up the house, and Mrs. Mullins gave me a rag as we started. "What's this for?" I asked.

"Well, I've covered this house over and over. I don't know how I could have missed the book. At least this way, even if we don't find my recipe book, we'll have dusted the house," she said and started off for the rooms she was to check. "Remember," she called over her shoulder, "the book is big, brown, and says *RECIPES* in gold."

At first, I was so sure that each drawer I opened would reveal the book that I didn't even mind sliding the dust cloth over everything, but an hour later I was still dusting, there was no sign of any book, and I was getting tired and bored. I didn't even dust at home. I began to wonder if there was no brown book at all, and this was just Mrs. Mullins's way of getting me to clean her house. Well, it might work today, but I wasn't going to fall for it again. That was for sure!

I passed the kitchen and realized that I hadn't had an after-school snack yet. I was going to have to ask my mom to send one to school with me, since it seemed that Mrs. Mullins didn't plan to offer me anything. My stomach grumbled, and I figured that it couldn't hurt if I stopped in and got a little something out of the refrigerator. Mrs. Mullins would never even know.

I'd just opened the door when I heard a voice behind me say, "I don't think you'll find my special book in the refrigerator. It doesn't need to be kept cold."

I jumped back. "I was, uh, I was just passing the refrigerator, and I was kind of hungry, so I thought I'd make myself a little snack. I guess I should have asked. Sorry. But I really have been looking hard. Look, my dust rag is even all dirty from dusting."

Mrs. Mullins walked toward me. I was dead if she told my mom that I'd gone into her refrigerator without asking. My mom was real big on politeness. Mrs. Mullins opened the refrigerator again. "Tssk, it really is quite empty. I simply must get to the store. All I've got for a snack is some kiwi fruit."

I thought kiwi was gross. "Oh, don't worry about it; I'm not really that hungry," I said. Then my dumb stomach turned me into a liar by growling again.

Mrs. Mullins looked at me firmly. "Obviously you are. Allan, you must tell me the truth. If you're going to be around, and it looks as if you are, you must not lie."

"Okay," I said meeting her gaze. "I'm very hungry. I'm used to getting a snack after school, and I hate kiwi."

"That's better. Actually I wouldn't mind a snack myself, and that kiwi isn't very good. Unfortunately my feet hurt too much to walk to the store today."

I looked at the pointy, black lace-up shoes she was wearing. "Well, if you'd wear tennis shoes like mine, instead of those, your feet wouldn't hurt." It was a gamble, but she said she wanted honesty.

Mrs. Mullins almost smiled. Then she pulled her face back into a normal look. "Well, I don't own tennis shoes like yours, and frankly, I'm not sure I want to. However, since my feet hurt too much to walk to the store, and I don't drive, I guess we'll just have to make some brownies here."

"That'd be fine," I said. "Do you want me to get the flour?"

"What flour?" asked Mrs. Mullins. "Why would I want flour?"

Oh, well, I thought to myself, so much for a snack. If she doesn't even know that flour goes into brownies, they're going to be pretty awful.

Suddenly Mrs. Mullins said, "Oh, for heaven's sake, you didn't actually think we were going to bake them, did you? Why, I always make brownies by magic."

"Wow! Okay, I mean, of course, you do," I said, telling myself to shut up before I said the wrong thing and Mrs. Mullins changed her mind.

"Watch me!" she commanded. Then she began talking to herself. "I just hope I remember how to do this one. I've done it hundreds of times before, but I'd sure feel better if I could check the spell against my magic book."

Even though I didn't believe in witches, and I wasn't really sure she could spin a spell, my heart was pounding and the tips of my fingers were positively tingling.

We walked into the kitchen, and Mrs. Mullins got out a big mixing bowl. For a minute, I felt real upset because I was sure that she was going to get flour and sugar and stuff and she'd just been teasing me about the magic. But she took down three strange powders from the cabinet by the sink and dumped a little of each into the bowl. "Well, combined with the right words, that should do it," she said.

I peered into the bowl. "Shouldn't you add a little chocolate?"

Mrs. Mullins pushed her glasses up on top of her white hair, closed her eyes, and began chanting something. I tried hard to figure out what she was saying, but she was going really fast and besides, it didn't sound as if she were talking in English at all. Suddenly it got very quiet. I stared at the bowl, Mrs. Mullins stared at the bowl, and . . . absolutely nothing happened.

I must admit, my heart sank right down to my feet. I should have known better than to honestly even consider believing that a person could cast spells. "Well," Mrs. Mullins began, "I just don't know. . . ." At that exact moment, there was a poof. Honest to goodness, as ridiculous as that sounds, there really was a poof, and there in the middle of Mrs. Mullins's kitchen table sat a little brown dog barking furiously.

My mouth fell open. "Oh dear, oh dear," Mrs. Mullins lamented. "Now, what did I do wrong?"

With a trembling hand, I reached out to comfort the terrified dog. As I petted him, he began to stop barking, and I saw that he was wearing a dog tag. Bending toward it, I read aloud, " 'My name is Brownie, 8754 W. Elm St., 555-1387.' "

"Mrs. Mullins!" I said joyfully. "You did it! You really did do it! I mean, it's not the kind of brownies you meant, but the dog's *name* is Brownie!" I looked at her and she looked at me and we both began to laugh.

"Oh, Allan, we'd better return him immediately. I certainly don't want anyone suspecting anything. Fortunately that address isn't too far from here. It's close enough that he might have just wandered over." She walked over to a kitchen drawer and began digging through it. "I don't have any kind of a leash, but I was sure I had some string in here somewhere."

"My belt, Mrs. Mullins, we can use my belt for a leash."

Mrs. Mullins came back to the table as I hurriedly removed my belt. It was lucky my mom had made me wear one this morning. "Good thinking, Allan! Let's get him back immediately."

In no time we had one end of the belt looped around the dog's collar and the other firmly in Mrs. Mullins's hand. Walking the few blocks to Brownie's house, we'd look at the dog, look at each other, and begin to laugh. "You know, Mrs. Mullins, your magic may be a little mixed-up, but it's a lot of fun," I told her.

Checking addresses when we got to W. Elm Street, we soon found 8754. It was a pretty pink house with a white fence around the outside. I opened the gate and held it open for Brownie and Mrs. Mullins. As we got to the front door, Brownie's tail began to wag furiously as if to say he was glad to be back home. I pushed the doorbell, and a tall lady with long dark hair opened the door almost immediately. Mrs. Mullins started to say, "We've come to return —"

But the lady interrupted her. "Oh, you've found Brownie! Thank heavens. I just can't figure out how he got out of the house. I'm always so careful not to leave the door open." She scooped Brownie up in her arms, and he began licking her face. "He's never run away before, and I was afraid he wouldn't be able to find his way home. Wherever did you find him?"

Mrs. Mullins looked at me and I looked at her. "Uh, actually, he just sort of popped up," I said, "and as soon as we saw his tag, we wanted to get him right back to you."

I bit the inside of my cheek to keep from laughing. He certainly had just popped up!

"I'm so grateful to you both. Let me give you a reward."

"Oh, no, that's not at all necessary," Mrs. Mullins said firmly. "It was our pleasure to return Brownie."

"If you won't take any money, at least let me

give you some of the chocolate chip cookies that I just finished baking."

My stomach growled again, and I certainly hoped Mrs. Mullins was going to accept the cookies. "That would be very nice of you, I'm sure," Mrs. Mullins said. I grinned.

Brownie's owner put at least a dozen still-warm cookies in a bag and thanked us again for returning him to her. We said it was no trouble, and as we said good-bye to the lady, I was almost sure that I saw Brownie wink at us.

I was holding my belt in my hands as we started back to Mrs. Mullins's house. "I guess I'd better put this on. My mom would never understand if I lost it."

Mrs. Mullins waited for me to finish and then took a cookie out of the bag for each of us. They were absolutely delicious, and we both munched in silent pleasure until we were almost back to her house. Frankly I couldn't remember when I'd ever enjoyed a snack more.

As we reached the walkway to Mrs. Mullins's house, she looked at the small gold watch she wore on a chain around her neck. "Well, Allan, though I can hardly believe it, it's already time for you to head on home. Your mother will be waiting for you."

"Right. Thanks for a great day!" I said. I meant

every word. I started to walk away, and Mrs. Mullins went into her house. Then I stopped, turned around, and ran back to her front door. I rang the bell. "Mrs. Mullins, Brownie really *did* just pop up on the kitchen table, didn't he?"

"Yes, Allan, I'm rather afraid that's exactly what he did."

"Great," I said. "That's absolutely great. I just needed to hear it again."

I smiled so much all the way home that my face almost hurt. What a great world it was. My mother kept remarking all through dinner that I seemed so happy, and that made her so happy. But it was her comment after dinner that put the final touch on the day. She said, "I stopped at the bakery to get us something special for dessert," and with that she put a plate of brownies on the table. I laughed so hard I almost fell off my chair, but despite my mother's perplexed asking of "what was so funny about a plate of brownies," I never said a single word.

5

It was awhile before Mrs. Mullins got around to doing more magic, and I guess you could say that it was partly my fault. Things started innocently enough. Mrs. Mullins picked up my backpack and commented that it was certainly heavy. I shouldn't have replied, but without even thinking of the possible consequences, I said, "That's because it's filled with lots of dumb stuff that I have to do for a report next week."

All of a sudden, Mrs. Mullins, who didn't know anything about kids and had never even baby-sat, started to sound like some kind of a teacher or mother. "Well, the report isn't going to get done by itself. You'd better work on it while you're here."

"But Mrs. Mullins . . ." I stopped protesting in midsentence. Magic! We could get the report written by magic. Why spend a week of time on it when someone like Mrs. Mullins could just mix a powder or two and poof, the report would be completely finished?

"Absolutely not!" Mrs. Mullins fumed when I suggested it. "I've never heard of anything so absurd. Do you think any self-respecting witch would agree to such a plan?"

I really had no idea. I didn't know any other witches, and I didn't see why Mrs. Mullins was becoming so unglued at the idea of a little magic to get me through my homework. Who wouldn't have liked the idea? But in spite of my most convincing arguments, Mrs. Mullins showed no mercy. I was to work on my report, and that was that. She seemed quite pleased with herself for taking a firm stand. However, just as I began to think there was no hope for her, I saw her green eyes glint, and she said, "Tell you what: You earn an A on that report on your own, and then we'll do a terrific little magic spell together."

I was definitely not pleased about having to work on some dumb report about Abraham Lincoln, but the idea of a terrific magic spell made it worth trying hard. Mrs. Mullins joined me at the kitchen table. She borrowed some of my notebook paper and tried to remember the recipes for different spells. At the end of our first day of work, we had a kitchen table full of wadded-up papers, and nothing accomplished. "Are you sure you don't want to just try using a spell for this report?

44

I mean, maybe you could send us both back in time; I could find Abraham Lincoln, and I could ask him what he wanted kids to write about him a hundred years after he was dead. It'd be great!"

My reasoning certainly sounded good to me, but it didn't seem to have any effect on Mrs. Mullins at all. About the only concession she made was to put out some store-bought cookies for us both, and milk for me and iced tea for her. With our refreshments next to us, the two of us sat at that kitchen table each day, and we each struggled with our own projects.

Finally my report was due, and I had to admit that it looked pretty good. It was the longest report I'd ever written in my whole life. When I showed it to my mom that night, she got all teary-eyed. "Oh, Allan, I'm so proud of you. Bless Mrs. Mullins's heart. How ever did she get you so motivated?"

"Uh, I don't know. I worked on my report, and she sat at the table and worked on some recipes."

The next day I handed it in to Miss Jenkins; she looked a little surprised. "Well, Allan . . ." she said, leafing through my report. "It looks as if you found out quite a bit about Mr. Lincoln." I took that to be a good sign.

Mrs. Mullins had had less luck with her project. She'd tried to remember and recopy ten different recipes for magic, but she felt certain that she hadn't gotten any of them exactly right.

Reporting to Mrs. Mullins, I tried to explain that it could be a very long time before Miss Jenkins graded my paper. "I'm sure she's going to like it. She practically said she did. Waiting to do magic until I get the paper back is going to be like waiting forever."

Mrs. Mullins wouldn't budge. "I miss the magic; I really do. I'm the one who's used to doing it. But we'll both wait to see the outcome of your report before we see any spells around this house."

I groaned. "Mrs. Mullins, can't you just be a witch?"

"I am a witch," she replied. "But I've decided that witches who get roped into baby-sitting better pay attention to their charge's homework."

Every day I'd get to school and the first thing I'd ask Miss Jenkins was whether our social studies papers had been graded yet. Finally she told me not to say another word. She'd let me know as soon as they were ready. Eventually the day did come for her to pass back the papers. First she handed back Karen Alexander's paper. Karen got an A. Karen always got an A, and so did Jennifer. I knew because Karen and Jennifer passed each other's papers across my desk. I watched Miss Jenkins walk up and down the rows. My heart was pounding, and the stack of papers was getting smaller. Johnny Rathing sat in front of me. He got a C on his paper, and I still didn't have mine back. If Miss Jenkins was handing them out by grade, I was dead. Finally she laid my paper on my desk. I was so nervous about it that I turned my paper facedown and couldn't make myself look at it until the final bell of the day had rung. Slowly I turned it over. I was peeking at it out of one eye. Then I saw the grade. It was an A−. "Whoopee!" I shouted, and some kids who were just leaving for the bus looked at me very strangely. Who cared about the minus part?! I'd gotten my first A in social studies all year, and to tell you the truth, it felt pretty good. Of course, some kid in a book might say that it felt so good to get an A that he didn't even care about the magic, but I wasn't some kid in a book. I was me, and I felt proud of myself, but not so proud that I didn't want to get on with the magic immediately. I practically ran to Mrs. Mullins's house.

The front door was unlocked, and I pushed it open quickly. "Mrs. Mullins, Mrs. Mullins!" I yelled.

"Here in the living room, Allan," she called. "Why are you shouting?"

I didn't even answer. I just yanked the paper from my backpack, and I put it on her lap. She picked it up and smiled. "You know, I'm a pretty good baby-sitter, after all!"

"Mrs. Mullins, let's get on with some magic!"

Mrs. Mullins stood up. "Very well. Goodness knows, I'm more than ready for a little magic. What did you have in mind?"

"I, uh . . . well . . . uh . . ." I'd been waiting for this day so long, and I'd thought of so many different possibilities that I couldn't decide what to choose.

Mrs. Mullins tapped her pointy shoe. "My fingers are just itching to get started with some magic. Tell me something right away or I'll choose."

"Okay," I said. "I've got it! Jennifer, this girl at school, she always bugs me. She's always trying to make me look dumb, and —"

"Yes," Mrs. Mullins interrupted. "What's that got to do with magic?"

"Well, I want you to make her hair turn purple and her body turn green, and I want it to happen right during spelling tomorrow." Boy, was that ever going to be neat. Little Miss Perfect turning colors in front of the whole class.

"Out of the question," Mrs. Mullins announced.

"But why —?"

Mrs. Mullins cut me off again. "First of all, it would be mean, and I don't feel like being mean. Second of all, it wouldn't be any fun for me; what good is it for me to do magic if I can't even see what happens? And third of all, and most important, as you know, I do *not* want anyone in this town to know I'm a witch. Now if a perfectly adorable ten-year-old girl turns purple and green, you can just bet there's going to be a big investigation. No thank you, Allan Hobart. That's a spell I won't even consider. Now, choose something simple, and something that we can see together. Choose something that won't affect anything outside this house, or choose nothing at all."

"Well, let me get a drink before I decide," I said, stalling while I thought. I wanted to choose just the right thing. I opened the refrigerator, and for a change, all Mrs. Mullins had was milk!

"Now, Allan. Choose right now!"

"I wish I had cherry soda pop to drink instead of milk!"

Mrs. Mullins pushed her glasses up on her nose. "That's the magic you want to do?"

I hadn't intended that, but it might just work. I looked at the sink. "Yeah. I want to turn on the kitchen sink and have it be cherry soda pop!"

"Well —" said Mrs. Mullins.

This time it was my turn to interrupt. "You said it had to be something that was just in this house, something that no one else would know about, something that we could see together, and something that was simple. So turning water into cherry soda pop works, doesn't it?"

Mrs. Mullins didn't say anything at first; she

49

just reached into the cabinet for her magic mixing bowl. "I haven't done anything like this in a long time," she said more to herself than to me. "Still, it was handy the time I gave a dinner party to have the tap dispense iced tea. This must be basically the same spell."

I volunteered to take notes on everything that Mrs. Mullins did. That way, if the spell worked, she'd have at least one correct recipe to start her spell book again. Mrs. Mullins moved pretty fast, and I had to write quickly. "There," she said, stepping proudly back from the bowl. "Give it a minute or two, and you should have cherry pop from the cold-water tap of the sink."

"Awesome!" I replied. "I'll get us some glasses." I took down two of the tallest glasses Mrs. Mullins had and walked over to the sink. "Now?" I asked her. "Now can I turn it on?"

Mrs. Mullins laughed. "Oh, it feels so good to do magic again! Let's see. This spell should give us about an hour of having the cherry soda instead of water."

"You mean it won't last forever?"

Mrs. Mullins laughed again. "Allan, I need water much more often than I need cherry pop, but this will be fun today. Turn on the faucet now, and get ready to celebrate our magic with a toast of cherry pop!"

I reached out my hand and turned on the faucet. "This is absolutely . . ." I stopped and stared. I stuck my finger under the spigot and then licked my fingertip. "Mrs. Mullins, it's still just water."

I don't know who was more disappointed, Mrs. Mullins or me. At first, she said that maybe we'd just tried it too soon, and we should wait a minute, so we waited, and then we tried again. I crossed the fingers of my left hand, then reached out and turned on the faucet with my right. Out came plain old water. I looked at Mrs. Mullins, and she looked ready to cry. "I don't understand it. I've never had a spell just not work at all. Sure, they may have gone a little wrong lately, but . . ." She sank down into a chair and got an awful look on her face. "Oh," she almost whispered, "what if something's happened to my witching power?"

I tried to think of the right thing or even anything to say. I mean, I felt real bad about not getting cherry soda pop from the faucet, but Mrs. Mullins felt as if she weren't even a witch any more. "Listen, Mrs. Mullins, why don't you try it again? I'm sure it would probably work if you just did it again."

Mrs. Mullins just shook her head. "A true witch always gets a result from a spell." I couldn't think of anything else to say. It got so quiet in the room it was almost spooky. Then I thought I heard a bell. The ringing sound happened again. "Mrs.

Mullins, that's your front door. Someone is here. Hey, maybe it's like Brownie, remember? Maybe, it's the pop man!" I got out of my chair and ran to the front door, throwing it open.

It wasn't the pop man. It wasn't even a big can of cherry soda. It was only Miss Switzer. Great, I thought. Just what we need right now — the busybody from next door. I stood at the door, but I didn't ask Miss Switzer to come in.

That didn't seem to bother her a bit. "Allan, do step aside," she commanded. "I must speak to Henrietta immediately."

I gulped, knowing that what I was about to say was probably going to get me in trouble later, but I just couldn't see letting Miss Switzer bother Mrs. Mullins when Mrs. Mullins was so upset. "I don't really think she wants company right now," I told Miss Switzer. "Why don't you come back tomorrow?"

Miss Switzer shot daggers at me. "Young man, where did you learn your manners? Now step aside. Henrietta? Henrietta?" she called as she marched into the house.

Mrs. Mullins walked into the living room. "Hello, Blanche." She didn't look any happier to see Miss Switzer than I was. Miss Switzer didn't even pay any attention. She just plopped herself down on the sofa. "Henrietta, the strangest . . ."

Then she stopped herself. "So, dear Henrietta, how *has* your afternoon been today?"

Mrs. Mullins sneaked a look at me, and I shrugged an "I-don't-know-what-Miss-Switzer-is-up-to" look back.

Trying to muster a smile, Mrs. Mullins said, "Actually Blanche, I'm a little tired today."

Miss Switzer sniffed. "Well, no wonder, trying to keep up with such a rude boy. Allan, go in and get me a glass of water. And hurry it up, please! I'm quite thirsty, and my water . . . is, is at my house, of course." I went into the kitchen and got Miss Switzer her water. When I brought it to her, she pinched my cheek, and said, "That's a good boy. Now, go play. It's not nice to intrude on adult conversation."

Boy, I hated people like Miss Switzer. I felt like telling her so, but I figured it might only make things hard on Mrs. Mullins, so I didn't say anything. I walked back in the kitchen and made a little wish. Oh, please, I thought. Please make it be cherry soda pop. I closed my eyes real tight while I wished, and then I opened them again and turned on the faucet. It still spurted out only water!

I sighed, sat down in the kitchen, and started to think. All of a sudden, I got this amazing idea. I peeked in the living room to make sure Miss

Switzer was still babbling on, then I quietly sneaked out the back door of Mrs. Mullins's house, climbed over her fence, and looked for an open window at Miss Switzer's. The next thing I knew I was standing in Miss Switzer's house. If she came home and caught me here, I'd be absolutely dead. My heart was pounding, but I didn't leave. I'd come with a mission. I ran to the kitchen, turned on the faucet, and just as I suspected, red soda pop poured out.

I wanted to laugh. I wanted to shout to Mrs. Mullins that she was still a witch, that we had done magic; it had just gotten a little bit mixed-up. I went through Miss Switzer's house turning on other faucets just to see how badly we'd messed up, and every faucet in the house poured forth cherry pop. No wonder she'd come to Mrs. Mullins's looking for a drink of water. No doubt she was also trying to find out if Mrs. Mullins's water was also cherry pop.

I knew just what I had to do. I did it, and then I returned. No one even realized I'd been gone. Finally Miss Switzer left. I could hardly wait for her to go. Mrs. Mullins looked relieved. "Oh, Allan, when things go wrong, they really go wrong. I thought she'd never leave, and to tell you the truth, I can't figure out what she wanted."

I tried not to laugh. "Come with me," I ordered Mrs. Mullins. We walked into the kitchen, and on the table were two big glasses of red soda pop.

"What on earth . . .?" Mrs. Mullins asked.

"Compliments of Miss Switzer."

Mrs. Mullins's green eyes grew very large. "You mean —?"

"Yes, yes," I interrupted. "You are still a witch. Your spell did work. It just worked at Miss Switzer's house." We both started to laugh as we imagined that stuffy old lady turning on every faucet in her house only to find they all poured out cherry soda pop.

"And the best part," I said, "is that by the time she gets home the spell will have worn off; the faucets will be filled with water, and Miss Switzer, who always knows everything, won't have a clue as to what happened."

"To you, Allan Hobart." Mrs. Mullins raised her glass of cherry soda pop, and we toasted. It was the very best soda I'd ever drunk.

6

A few days later, I told Mrs. Mullins, "I've got a great idea. I think we should get some cherry soda pop and leave it on Miss Switzer's doorstep. It would drive her crazy!"

"Allan, that is out of . . ."

I interrupted. "Oh, don't say no, Mrs. Mullins, think about it. She barged right into your house, made herself at home, and then called me a rude boy. Besides, she's always acting like such a know-it-all."

Mrs. Mullins smiled. "Well, she is a bit of a busybody, but that's even more reason that we don't want to start her asking questions." Mrs. Mullins sighed deeply, and stared off into space. I was pretty sure she was thinking about her old neighborhood again. She always got this real sad look on her face when she talked about her old house. I knew just how she felt. She missed it, but she couldn't ever go back to live there again, and it really wasn't her fault. It was like the way

I missed my dad, and even though I really wanted it to happen, I knew I could never make Mom and Dad live together again.

Then it hit me hard. Why hadn't I thought of it before? Of course, *I* couldn't do anything, but Mrs. Mullins. . . . My words started tripping all over each other. "I know what magic we should do next! We've got to get started right away."

Mrs. Mullins pushed a strand of loose hair up into her bun. "Allan, what's gotten in to you?"

"Come on, Mrs. Mullins!" I grabbed her hand to pull her into the kitchen. "You're going to make my mom and dad fall in love again. The Hobarts are going to be a family again!"

I ran into the kitchen and threw open the cupboard doors. "Which of this terrific white stuff do we use?"

Mrs. Mullins came in after me, and when I turned to look at her, I didn't like the expression on her face. "Mrs. Mullins, you can't say no; this time you just can't. It's too important. You can't imagine what it's like to have your dad leave one day. Sure, he tells you he still loves you, and your mom tells you she still loves you, but nothing is the same. Oh, please, Mrs. Mullins."

I guess somehow I kind of had tears on my cheeks because Mrs. Mullins walked up and wiped them with a Kleenex. "Allan, if I could do that for you, I would. I really would. But I don't have any magic spell to make people love each other. They have to figure out how to do that on their own. But I am sure of this. I've talked to your mom, and I know there's nothing on earth as strong as her love for you. I'm certain that your dad really loves you, too. So even though there is no magic spell to put your parents back together, there's also no magic spell that's ever strong enough to break the love each of them feels for you."

I walked out of the kitchen real fast. I knew that fourth-graders were too old to cry, but I just couldn't help it. I sat by myself in the living room for a long time. Finally Mrs. Mullins came in. I think we both felt kind of embarrassed. It was real quiet. I knew I didn't want to talk about Mom and Dad anymore, and staring out the window, I said, "You know, Mrs. Mullins, you might like your house better if you had some pretty flowers out in front."

"Allan, that's a perfect idea; I don't know why I didn't think of it! At my old house, I had tons of flowers in the front yard."

I smiled. "Mrs. Mullins, how well do you remember your flower spell?"

"Oh, I'm pretty sure . . ." She stopped herself. "Actually Allan, I'm afraid we'd better plant the flowers the way ordinary people do."

"Awww, you mean just buy them and put them in the ground?"

Mrs. Mullins nodded yes. "Allan, I'm not sure about the spell. I can't risk trying to create flowers in the front yard, and having them turn out to be . . . well, who knows what they'd be. I'll buy some flowers while you're at school tomorrow. Will you help me plant them?"

I said I would. I mean, what else could I do, after Mrs. Mullins had tried so hard to make me feel better about Mom and Dad? Still, it wasn't exactly my idea of a great way to spend an afternoon. I almost hoped that it would rain, but wouldn't you know it, the day was sunny and just fine for planting flowers. I didn't exactly rush toward Mrs. Mullins's, but I got there just the same. "Jeez!" I said as I approached her front walk. It was obvious that Mrs. Mullins had taken this flower thing real seriously, since there were about a million of them waiting to be planted.

I walked in the front door. Mrs. Mullins was humming slightly off-key in the kitchen. "Allan, is that you?" she called. "Come here."

I walked into the kitchen, and there were two chocolate donuts. "For you," she gestured. "I got them while I was out buying the flowers. And I'm so glad we thought of flowers. They're just what this house needs."

"I'm not sure the whole block needs as many flowers as you bought," I said, and then I saw Mrs. Mullins's feet. I looked, and then I looked again. "I don't believe it!" I exclaimed, as I watched Mrs. Mullins walk across the room.

"Believe what?" she asked.

"Your shoes!" I exclaimed. I mean, she was the same white-haired, spectacled, flowered-dress Mrs. Mullins, except that instead of her normal black pointy shoes, she was wearing a pair of red high-top sneakers just like mine.

"Like them?" She stuck out one foot. "I decided you were right. Those other shoes were ugly and uncomfortable. These may still be ugly, but they are certainly very comfortable!"

I shook my head, and to keep from laughing, grabbed a donut, and stuffed it in my mouth.

Mrs. Mullins and I spent all afternoon planting her flowers. We put them by the house, we lined the walkway with flowers, and we even put a few around the mailbox. It wasn't as bad as I'd thought it would be, and everything did look nice when we finished. Now all they had to do was grow.

The only problem was that they didn't grow at all. In fact, within a week, they started to die. The bright colors of the flowers were beginning to shrivel into little dead balls. I hated to see all my hard work go for nothing, and Mrs. Mullins wasn't too pleased herself. That's why after ten days of trying all the ordinary ways to get flowers to grow and failing, she decided that we could try a little magical growing powder on the flowers. "But just a very little, and on just a very few flowers," she warned.

The growing powder did seem to perk the flowers up a little bit. Now they only looked half-dead instead of almost dead, so I convinced Mrs. Mullins that we needed more and a little stronger formula. "After all, we know that it works now!" I persuaded Mrs. Mullins.

She had to think about it for a few minutes. "For heaven sakes," I complained. "You're the most cautious witch I've ever met!"

Mrs. Mullins fixed me with a look. "I'm the *only* witch you've ever met, and besides, you don't believe in witches, remember?" Having made her point, she walked into the kitchen, smiling. "Well, aren't you coming?" she called. "After all, it was your suggestion to make a second batch of this stuff."

Mrs. Mullins worked quickly measuring and stirring, and it was practically no time before we had a big second batch of the special growing powder. "It feels so good to have a magic spell that I know works right," she said. "Now, let's go get those flowers to grow." She picked up the bowl, and the phone rang. Mrs. Mullins sighed. "I'll get the phone; you start sprinkling the solution on the flowers."

I was just walking out of the house with the bowl in my hand when I heard her say, "Oh, hello, Blanche. . . ."

I took the white powder and sprinkled it on the flowers, but it didn't look as if much was happening. I was almost finished when I saw Jeff Wilson a few houses down the street. He was kicking a stone, and he looked pretty bored, so I put my bowl down and called his name. He waved and somehow, I kicked over the bowl. Thank goodness, it didn't break or anything, and there hadn't been much powder left in it before it spilled. The bowl looked okay. Mrs. Mullins wouldn't be mad, and the flowers had had enough growing powder. I yelled, "Hey, Jeff, want to play catch?"

My heart was pounding. I mean, Jeff and I knew each other at school, but he was always the star, and everyone wanted to play catch with him. I almost wished I hadn't said anything, but it was too late. Jeff walked toward me, and I couldn't tell what he was thinking. "Allan, am I ever glad to see you!" he said when he got to me.

"You are?"

"Yeah, we're visiting my cousins, and all they've got is two little babies. It's real boring. I'll go get my glove. You have a glove, too, don't you?"

"Sure, yeah, uh, I do." Boy, I sounded like a jerk, but I was so nervous. I ran in to stick the bowl in the house, get my glove from my back-pack, and tell Mrs. Mullins that I was going out to play catch. She was still listening on the phone, so I held up my glove, and I ran outside. Part of me could hardly wait and part of me was scared to death to play catch with the best baseball player at Miller.

When I got back outside, Jeff was tossing the baseball in the air and catching it in his mitt. "Okay, here's an easy warm-up."

"Oh, please," I prayed as the ball came toward me, "don't let me drop this." *Kerplunk*. The ball landed in my glove and it felt terrific.

We tossed the ball for a few minutes, and I didn't drop one. Then Jeff said, "Go farther back, and let's play some *real* catch. Throw 'em as hard as you can!"

I moved way back and soon a flying white speck was headed my way. It hit my glove so hard that my hand stung. I threw a pop fly back to him. He dived for it and missed.

"Hey, nice going. That was a great throw." He slammed the ball back at me, and I caught it again! We played hard for about forty minutes, and I only missed five balls, which wasn't bad considering even Jeff had missed two.

Finally we decided to take a break. Sitting on the sidewalk, Jeff said, "You've got a pretty good arm. Are you a Cubs' fan?"

"Yeah! I've got a cap that my dad brought back from one of the games in Chicago."

"Really? That's great. Do you collect baseball cards?"

"Sure, I just got an Andre Dawson and a Greg Maddux —"

Jeff interrupted. "Greg Maddux is one I really want to get. He's got some arm! What a blazing fastball!" Jeff rubbed his hand. "Hey, how come you never throw the ball hard at school?"

I shrugged. "I don't know. I guess I tense up or something."

Jeff's mom started calling him. "Well, I guess I gotta go. We'll have to play catch again some-time. You're not bad. See ya at school."

I was so happy I could hardly stand it. To be called not bad by the best baseball player at Miller Elementary was no small compliment! I ran inside to tell Mrs. Mullins all about it, and by the time I'd gotten done explaining every throw, it was time for me to go home.

I saw Jeff the next morning at school, but he was with a gang of his usual buddies, and he didn't say anything to me, so I didn't say anything to him. I wondered if he even remembered that we'd ever played catch.

Just like always, Jeff got to be captain of one PE baseball team, and Steve, the other. "Okay, choose sides," the coach called.

"Hobart," Jeff called for his first pick.

"Me?" I sort of squeaked, and Steve looked like Jeff was crazy.

"What are you doin' today," Steve asked, "tryin' to give the game away?"

Jeff laughed. "I never give baseball games away."

I walked over to Jeff's side. "You're playing catcher. Just be as good as you were yesterday," he muttered to me.

I really wasn't sure I could do that. Yesterday might have been a fluke. I might make our whole team lose the game. "Listen, Jeff," I said, "I'd really rather play in the outfield like usual."

Jeff looked at me strangely. "Okay, suit yourself. Cook, you play catcher."

Our team won the game just as the school dismissal bell rang, but I didn't have anything to do with the win. No balls had even come to my position clear out in the outfield. Sighing, I wondered what would have happened if I'd had the nerve to play catcher. I walked toward Mrs. Mullins's house. Maybe Jeff would be at his cousins' house again, and we could play catch. Then maybe after a few more times of playing catch, Jeff would say that he was sure I'd be a great catcher. And when he picked me, I'd know I could do it, and then our team would win the game!

I rushed toward Mrs. Mullins's. Please, Jeff, be

at your cousins', I thought. But when I got to the right block, I couldn't see Jeff; I couldn't even see Mrs. Mullins's house. Cars lined the streets. The Channel 10 television news truck looked as if it were parked right in front of Mrs. Mullins's house.

Uh, oh, I thought to myself. I looked around, and then I looked up, and up, and up. "Oh, no," I whispered under my breath, and I ran toward Mrs. Mullins's.

When I got to her house, I saw the television man sticking a microphone in her face. "Good afternoon, ladies and gentlemen, here's a Channel 10 news update. We are live at the home of Henrietta Mullins, where we are seeing a ten-foot daisy. Mrs. Mullins, can you explain this strange happening?"

I held my breath. This was all my fault! The powder that I'd spilled yesterday! And I hadn't even remembered to tell Mrs. Mullins what I'd done.

The man with the microphone continued to hold it in front of Mrs. Mullins and wait for an answer. What would she say? Would everyone know Mrs. Mullins was a witch? I saw Mrs. Mullins push her glasses up on her nose and begin to speak. Oh, Mrs. Mullins, I'm so sorry! I thought as I crossed my fingers and listened.

"Well, young man," she said to the reporter, "to tell you the truth, I've never seen anything like this daisy before. It's quite amazing. I just don't understand it at all. I bought some flowers at Gardeners' Nursery the other day, and I planted them all as you can certainly see. But I don't honestly know why this strange one is the way it is. Do you have any idea?" Mrs. Mullins looked the absolute picture of innocence, just a sweet, little old lady who was confused by this strange twist of nature.

The TV newsman seemed anxious to reassure her that everything would be okay. The camera turned off, and he said, "It's really quite attractive. I'm sure the botany department at the local university will find an answer, but even if they don't, it's nothing you need to worry about." He patted Mrs. Mullins's hand and ordered his crew, "Let's wrap it up and go."

The news truck took off, and so did a lot of the people. I breathed a sigh of relief. Then I realized Miss Blanche Switzer was standing behind me. Under her breath, I could hear her muttering to herself, "Strange things have been happening around here lately, that they have. Cherry pop instead of water, daisies ten feet tall. I mean to find out why."

7

As soon as the crowd was gone, Miss Switzer made a beeline for Mrs. Mullins. "Henrietta, do you know what I think —?"

Mrs. Mullins cut her short. "Excuse me, Blanche. I just can't talk right now. Allan has arrived, and I've got to get him started on his homework.

"Allan," she said sternly, "come inside with me right now!" Her eyes barely contained her anger.

Blanche stood on the sidewalk watching us go in, and as soon as the door shut so that she couldn't still see us, I expected Mrs. Mullins to start screaming. I wouldn't even have blamed her, but she didn't scream. Instead, she looked me straight in the eye, tapped her foot, and said nothing.

For one little minute, I began to wonder if she were going to turn me into a rabbit or something. I mean, it probably was not the smartest thing in the world to make a real witch mad. I stared back at her, trying to make some words come out of my mouth. She didn't look much like a wicked witch; she looked like a scared person who thought she might have to move again. I felt just awful. I sat down in the living room, and I just let the whole story spill out of me about accidentally kicking the bowl, and not telling her because she was on the phone, and forgetting later because I was excited about Jeff. "And that about wraps it up." I was afraid to even look at Mrs. Mullins.

"Well," she said, "I'm definitely not pleased."

"I'm really sorry —"

"On the other hand," she interrupted, "it is somewhat of a relief."

"It is? I mean, of course it is. I mean, why is it a relief?" I was stumbling all over my words. "I thought you'd be really mad."

"I didn't have a chance to be angry. I was too busy being worried. I didn't know why that daisy grew, and I thought all of them might soon be that big. Then we'd have had every national television station here, too, and it would have only been a matter of days until the whole country found out I was a witch. Then I couldn't have lived anywhere. At least I know that no other daisy is going to grow, and I've got one spell that works the way it's supposed to, providing no one spills a whole bowlful in a single spot on the ground."

I got the point and promised to be extra-extra careful if Mrs. Mullins would ever trust me again.

She didn't say whether she would or she wouldn't. She only murmured that she thought she needed a good, strong cup of hot tea and headed to the kitchen to boil some water.

For the next week or so, cars drove by her house every day. Some people got out of their cars and had their picture taken next to the daisy tree. The botany professor from the university downstate came to Mrs. Mullins's house and studied the tree. Finally he announced some complicated thing about genetics and recessive and dominant traits. Mrs. Mullins and I didn't understand one word he said. I don't think anyone else in town did, either, but they all decided that as long as the scientist had figured it out, it must be okay, and finally life on Mrs. Mullins's street went back to normal.

As a matter of fact, it was really very boringly normal. Mrs. Mullins didn't offer to do any more magic with me around. I could sort of see why, but I hadn't meant to cause all that trouble. Every day, as I walked to her house, I'd think of great ways I was going to ask her to do magic. Then I'd see the daisy tree in the front yard and totally lose my nerve to say anything.

Things were not exactly going great at school, either. Jeff hadn't shown up at his cousins' house again, and he hadn't picked me first again, either. I was just the nobody out in the outfield. Jennifer

Swanson, who seemed to specialize in making my life miserable, had been working overtime. She never missed a chance to get in another dig. Usually, I just tried to ignore her, but today I'd walked right into her trap. She'd just pushed me one time too much, and I'd made a promise to the class that I couldn't begin to keep. By the way she giggled, Jennifer knew she'd gotten me but good.

I stomped into Mrs. Mullins's house and threw my backpack on the floor. She'd been curled up in her green lounge chair in the living room reading a book, and she looked up with a start when she heard the thud. "Well, that's not much of a greeting. What's wrong with you?"

"I'm mad, really mad!"

"So I gathered," Mrs. Mullins said. "Something go wrong at school today?"

"It sure did, and it's called Jennifer Swanson."

"And just what did Jennifer Swanson do?"

"I don't want to talk about it," I said and I plopped myself down in a chair in the living room. "Dumb, stupid girl," I mumbled under my breath.

Mrs. Mullins took off her glasses and put down her book. "Allan, are you sure you don't want to talk about it?"

"I'm sure," I said through gritted teeth. "You should just be glad you never had to go to school with Jennifer Swanson."

"Umm, I went to school with Hank Craneshaw. That was bad enough."

"Yeah," I said, "well, I'll bet Hank Craneshaw never embarrassed you in front of your whole class."

Mrs. Mullins walked over to me, and she put her hand on my shoulder. "Allan, are you sure that you don't want to talk about this? It might make you feel better."

I took a deep breath and began to explain how Miss Jenkins had announced an end-of-project party, and how she'd drawn names from a hat to choose what each person should bring. "I kept hoping I wouldn't draw refreshments because that brat, Jennifer, brought the most incredible gingerbread men in for our last snack, and I knew she'd make fun of whatever I'd bring, since Mom doesn't really have time to bake. Anyway, what did I draw to bring in for this party . . . ? You guessed it, refreshments!"

I took my baseball cap off and began playing with it as I continued talking to Mrs. Mullins. I said that I'd waited until Miss Jenkins wasn't busy, and then I'd walked up to her desk to see if she thought I could switch and bring something besides food. But Miss Jenkins said to just bring in a couple of bags of Oreo cookies, and that would be fine. Jennifer, who sat right near the teacher's desk, overheard, groaned, and whispered to the whole class, "Our snack is going to be gross. Allan's bringing Oreos, and he always licks the middle before he gives them out."

A bunch of her friends made faces and went, "Oooh, how gross!"

Then Miss Jenkins said, "Now, Jennifer, we mustn't tease that way."

Jennifer opened her big blue eyes and replied, "Oh, Miss Jenkins, I didn't mean to tease at all. Allan can't help it if no one in his house can bake." The class started to laugh.

There I was, Allan Hobart, the rotten baseball player, rotten snack maker. Something snapped, and I turned to Jennifer saying, "Don't you worry, my snack is going to be great . . . a lot better than those dumb gingerbread men you brought."

Maybe it was a couple of guys encouraging, "Right on!" but the next thing I knew my mouth was racing lots faster than my brain and I added, "Listen, everybody, I promise you this. My end-of-project snack is going to be the best one that anyone in this whole class has ever seen."

"Mrs. Mullins, you should have seen her gingerbread men. Each one was decorated perfectly, and they tasted wonderful. How can I ever top that?" I looked at the floor.

Mrs. Mullins tapped her tennis-shoed foot quickly. "I do declare. That unpleasant little girl does sound just like my Hank Craneshaw. Boy, he was mean! Why are there some children who take such delight in making life miserable for others!" Mrs. Mullins got up and began pacing the room. "Well, the question is, how are we going to let you keep your promise to the class?"

I really didn't think there was any way, but somehow at least it felt a little better to know Mrs. Mullins was on my side. We thought about baking, but Mrs. Mullins was a terrible baker, and I was no better. I mean, we might have been able to mix a batch of chocolate chip cookies, but I'd opened my mouth and told the class this was going to be the best snack ever, and chocolate chip cookies were not exactly unique.

"Maybe we'd better give it a try by magic," Mrs. Mullins suggested.

I sucked in my breath with excitement. It was the first time Mrs. Mullins had mentioned magic to me since the daisy tree incident in the front yard. Then I started to laugh. I didn't mean to. It just burst out. I remembered the time that we'd tried for brownies and ended up with the neighbor's dog, and I suddenly saw us trying to bake for the class and ending up with all the neighborhood dogs on Mrs. Mullins's kitchen table.

Mrs. Mullins was deep in thought and either didn't hear or didn't want to hear why I was laughing. "I wonder," she said aloud, "if I could remember my Cookie Grand spell?"

"What's a Cookie Grand?" I said curiously.

But Mrs. Mullins wouldn't tell me. She said she needed to think the spell through, and we'd try it after school the next day. I noticed that her green eyes were shining, and she looked happier than she had in weeks.

I wasn't going to say anything at school the next day. I really wasn't. Then at lunch, Jennifer and Karen sat across from me. Jennifer whispered in a real loud voice, "Wonder if Allan has any Oreos in his lunch that he's going to lick."

"Shut up, Jennifer," I replied. "You're a stupid jerk!"

Just then the lunch monitor walked by. "Allan Hobart, that kind of language isn't necessary." Jennifer waited until the monitor had walked on, and then she stuck her tongue out at me.

Finally school was out. I hurried to Mrs. Mullins's house, eager to get to making a Cookie Grand. "Mrs. Mullins," I called before I'd even gotten completely through the front door, "what's a Cookie Grand?"

"Come in the kitchen," she said, and I raced in. I noticed that she had a bowl of potion sitting in the middle of the table. "Now, Allan, don't get your hopes up. I'm not at all sure this is going to work, but if it does, there'll be a chocolate chip cookie as big as this table. I bought these little frosting decorators in the store, and I figure we could write the names of all the children in your class in icing on the top. What do you think?"

I looked at the table. If a cookie were that big, it would truly be gigantic. "I think it's going to be perfect. Thanks, Mrs. Mullins. Jennifer could never top it. Besides, I know the spell will work," I said firmly.

One thing was for sure, I'd already made up my mind that if everything today failed, and I had to walk into school tomorrow with two bags of Oreos, I was just not going to school at all.

My thoughts were interrupted. "Allan, you're not listening to me. Write the names of all of the children in your class on this piece of paper." I did so quickly. "Now close your eyes and hope." Mrs. Mullins began to chant softly and then louder. "Ifshcol, ago, and scrapmsd, although, by geit and boblio."

Please work, please work, please work, I thought to myself, hoping that maybe my wishes would help the spell succeed.

Suddenly I felt myself whirling through the air. "Mrs. Mullins," I called through a hazy red fog, "are you there? I really feel like we're moving."

There was no answer, but a minute later, I hit the ground with a thump. "Oooh," said Mrs. Mullins's voice, "that was a rough landing. At my age, I can't take too many of those."

I ran over to help her. "Are you okay? What happened, Mrs. Mullins, did we make a cookie so big that it knocked us down? Why can't I see anything?"

The fog was starting to clear. "I can see that we're still in your kitchen," and then I gasped as thunderous footsteps approached us. And before you could even say "Let me out of here!" a huge dark-brown giant was glaring down at us.

"What have we here?" he shouted, and the walls shook. "I don't appreciate getting knocked right out of my house!"

"Mind your manners, Allan," Mrs. Mullins whispered, and drawing herself to her feet, she said, "We're sorry if we've disturbed you. I'm Henrietta Mullins and this is my friend Allan Hobart. We were trying to create a Cookie Grand."

"What? I can't hear you." He leaned down.

"Yikes, Mrs. Mullins, run. He's going to eat us!"

Mrs. Mullins looked at me. "Well, if that's what he chooses to do, I don't think we're in much of a position to stop him, but just because he's so big doesn't mean that he's not friendly." The giant was now only about two inches away from us, and though it was a crazy time to think about it, I was sure I smelled wonderful chocolate. Mrs. Mullins cupped her hand to her mouth and shouted her greeting again.

"Cookie Grand?" he replied with a shout. "Why, do I look like a cookie?" Suddenly he barked, "Why did you think I wanted to be hurled into your kitchen? It was a rude thing to do!"

I figured it was only a matter of time until he ate us. Maybe I could at least save Mrs. Mullins. "It wasn't her idea," I shouted. "I made her do it."

"Oh, is that so? Why?"

I was going to make up some terrific story, but my knees were knocking and my heart was pounding, and all I could think of was the truth. So, as stupid as it sounded, I told him about Jennifer Swanson. His face was only inches away from mine, and it was the most gigantic face I'd ever seen. Every part of it was brown, even his eyes.

"She doesn't sound like a very nice little girl to me." The giant's voice thundered off the ceiling, and I wished she could hear him say so. I was sure he could give Jennifer a good scare.

"Well, she isn't, but it looks as if she's won again. Since we didn't make a Cookie Grand, I'll go back to class tomorrow with no refreshments at all, and she ought to have a wonderful time making fun of me."

"No!" stormed the giant, and I was sure he was going to say that he planned to eat us right away, so I didn't have to worry about ever going anywhere again. He looked at me, and I figured that meant I was getting eaten first. "Do you know every kid's name in your class?"

"Y-y-yeah, I think so," I said.

I wondered if he planned to eat me and Mrs. Mullins and then start in on the rest of my class. I watched him carefully. He took out a white file and began to file one of his fingertips to a fine point. Shavings from his nails began to fall around us, and, honest, they smelled just like chocolate.

I tried to work up my courage. "What, what are you going to do?"

"Watch and see," he commanded. He squinted his eyes. "Now, spell your name." I did, and to my amazement, he began to write my name with his fingernail. When he'd finished, he squinted to see his work. "Well, what do you think?" he asked, and he actually smiled a giant smile.

"It . . . it looks like . . . I mean it smells like . . ." I hoped I wasn't wrong. "It looks like you just wrote my name in chocolate."

"That's right!" He looked very proud of himself. "Don't you know who I am?"

"No sir, I'm sorry, but I don't."

Scrunching up against the ceiling he tried to stand to his full ten feet, announcing, "I am Chocolate Man. There is none other in the world like me. Made of thousands of pounds of the finest chocolate, I can reproduce the most delicate semi-sweet chocolate roses to the biggest milk choco-

79

late bunnies." He held up his right hand. "Here in my index finger, I have a never-ending supply of chocolate."

My mouth fell open. Sneaking a quick look at Mrs. Mullins, I saw that she was pretty amazed, too. So even witches didn't know about Chocolate Man.

"Well, I'm pleased to meet you," I said, "and I really want to thank you for this chocolate bar that spells my name. It's the neatest sweet treat I've ever seen."

"Well, thank you. For such a little person, you're pretty smart. Now I suppose I'd better get going if I've a whole class to do."

"A whole class?" I shouted. "You're going to write everyone's name in my class in chocolate?"

Chocolate Man smiled again. "I don't much like snippy little girls named Jennifer."

"You mean Jennifer Swanson?"

He began to write her name in chocolate. I imagined the look on her face when she saw these chocolate bars, and I began to laugh. She'd never tease me again. It only took Chocolate Man a few minutes before the names of all thirty kids in my class and Miss Jenkins were spelled out in chocolate. "Wow," I said in awe. "How can I ever thank you? This is going to be the neatest snack that anyone ever brought to Miller Elementary."

"I'm sure it will be," said Chocolate Man, "and

if you want to thank me, please, just get me home again now! I've got serious chocolate-making to do! Since I don't know exactly how I got here, I don't exactly know how to get home, so . . ." His big brown face looked confused.

It wasn't that we didn't want to say thanks a lot and send him on his way, but we had no idea how to do that. If all that weren't bad enough, we suddenly heard, "Yoo hoo, Henrietta, it's Blanche. I knocked, but no one answered, so I just came right in. Are you in the kitchen? Something smells delicious. I simply must come see what you're doing."

The chocolate giant took up most of the kitchen. There was no way we could hide him, even if he were willing to cooperate, and he looked less cooperative by the minute. Mrs. Mullins and I looked at each other in a state of total panic. "I'll think of something to do with Miss Switzer," I whispered frantically. "You try to figure out what to do with Chocolate Man."

I took a deep breath and walked out of the kitchen. "Shh," I whispered to Miss Switzer, thinking that I'd better think of something spectacular, or Mrs. Mullins and I were doomed.

Miss Switzer sniffed at me as if I were some disgusting little bug. "Allan, it is impolite to hush one's elders. When will you learn some manners?"

"Oh, I'm so sorry, Miss Switzer." I tried to look

my sweetest. "You're right. You must . . . you must sit down and let me really apologize."

"Well, I . . ."

"Here, Miss Switzer, sit right here. Let me tell you what I'm trying to do to be good these days." I started saying just anything. Miss Switzer listened for a while, but then she stood up, saying, "All right, Allan, that's enough. I'm glad you're trying to improve, but you do have a long way to go. Now excuse me. I have things to discuss with Mrs. Mullins."

"Oh, but you can't go in there!" I shouted in panic. Miss Switzer marched past me.

I felt like sinking into a chair and crying. It was all over. When Miss Switzer saw Chocolate Man, the whole town would know about it right away. Combined with the daisy tree in front of the house, the Chocolate Man episode would mean Mrs. Mullins would have to move again. I was going to lose a good friend. I fought tears, thinking somehow I should have made things work out better. But it was too late now. I watched in horror as Miss Switzer opened the door to the kitchen.

8

I forced myself to follow her into the kitchen. The least I could do was not leave Mrs. Mullins alone to face Miss Switzer and the giant.

When I walked through the door, I started to say, "I can explain —" and Miss Switzer interrupted me. "Allan, don't get involved in adult conversation. Now, Henrietta, as I was saying, these chocolate names are just fantastic. They are the cutest things I've ever seen. I want to know exactly how you did this. I'm going to write every word down. By the way, did I tell you that you spoil that child? Why ever did you tell me you couldn't bake?" She peered at Mrs. Mullins, intently waiting for an answer.

I allowed my eyes to sweep the kitchen. No giant! I didn't know how or where Mrs. Mullins had gotten rid of Chocolate Man, but I was hugely relieved.

Miss Switzer continued to prod Mrs. Mullins for the exact way to make the chocolate bars. "Really,

Blanche, I'm not much of a baker. I'd like to share the recipe, but . . ." Mrs. Mullins stopped as if she couldn't figure out quite what to say next.

I jumped in. "It's okay, Mrs. Mullins. Go ahead and tell her. Miss Switzer will understand. You see, Mrs. Mullins told me that this is an old family recipe, and Mrs. Mullins's mother made her promise never to give it away. That's why I couldn't even watch her bake, and I'm just a kid."

Miss Switzer didn't look too pleased, but she didn't argue, either. "Well, I suppose that everyone has some family traditions. Speaking of family, I'm going to Ingleside Inlet to visit my sister in just a few days." Miss Switzer's voice took on a tone of importance. "Do you know that my sister says a *witch* used to live in the very next town to hers! What do you think of that? I can tell you this: *I* certainly wouldn't tolerate any witches living anywhere at all around me! Why, I'd get rid of them and quick!"

Mrs. Mullins didn't say anything, but I could see how pale she had gotten. Finally, after Miss Switzer had talked for a while longer, she left. "Okay," I said, "first things first. Where's the giant?"

Mrs. Mullins sank into one of the kitchen chairs. "I was trying to explain that I couldn't send him home because I didn't exactly know what I was doing when I brought him here. He was getting really upset. In fact, I was sure he was going to go storming into the living room at any minute. I opened my magic powder cabinet to show him how things had happened. He grunted 'Ettimm!' picked up one of the powders, took a cupful, swallowed it, and the next thing I knew, he'd just disappeared. It was none too soon, either. Blanche Switzer walked through the door not thirty seconds later."

"Wow!" I said. "Talk about a close call!" I looked at the table. The chocolate bars were still there. I laughed out loud. "We did it! Miss Switzer didn't see Chocolate Man; I've got the greatest refreshments in the world, and . . ." I didn't want it to sound corny or anything so I looked at the floor when I said it. "And the neatest witch for a friend that anyone could ever hope to have."

Mrs. Mullins hugged me, and for some reason, I didn't mind at all.

That night, I took the chocolate bars home, and my mother thought they were wonderful. "That dear, sweet woman!" she exclaimed. "Oh, Allan, wasn't it fortunate that you didn't want to stay home alone, and that I went to see Mrs. Mullins! I'll bet your friends are just going to love these chocolate bars. Someday, when I finally get some extra time, I'll have to ask Mrs. Mullins for her recipe."

Mom was right about my friends' reactions. I

will never forget taking the chocolate bars to school. On that morning, Jennifer waited until the teacher was out of earshot and then made mean comments about the dog food cookies that I probably had in my refreshment box. I just didn't say a word until it was time to open the box. When the kids realized that their names were written in chocolate, everyone crowded around my desk. Even Miss Jenkins said she'd never seen anything quite like them, and she'd been teaching for fifteen years. Some kids ate their candy names right away and were absolutely sure it was the best chocolate they'd ever eaten; other kids said they were saving their special chocolate bars to show their parents. No one said a word about Jennifer's gingerbread men.

I'd decided to eat my chocolate a little at a time. I was going to save the A out of my name forever, but each day, I ate half of one of the other letters. Mrs. Mullins and I would take the chocolate out of the refrigrator and cut off a piece.

In the long run, the candy bars did and didn't change things at school. Jennifer Swanson still hated me, and she still gave me a hard time whenever she could, but for some reason, her disgusting teasing never quite bothered me as much again.

What *did* bother me, and it bothered Mrs. Mullins a whole lot more, was Miss Switzer. We talked and talked about it, but we just couldn't decide whether Miss Switzer had been hinting that she knew Mrs. Mullins was a witch.

One thing we did know for sure. Blanche Switzer was the worst gossip in the whole town. We didn't know what her sister in Ingleside Inlet would tell her, which is the reason that, though we were glad to have Miss Switzer out of town, we were plenty worried about what might happen when she returned. Mrs. Mullins paced the living room. "I can't believe Blanche's sister lives right near where I used to live. What if her sister describes the witch, and Blanche realizes the description looks just like me? I simply can't give her any further opportunity to get suspicious. I'll just have to stop doing magic." She shook her head sorrowfully. "How can a witch stop doing magic? It's what she's supposed to do."

I'd never seen Mrs. Mullins so upset, and it didn't seem to matter what I said. Nothing made her feel better. I sat in my room one night after dinner and tried to think it all out. Mrs. Mullins had to do magic. I was afraid she'd die without it. Yet she couldn't keep doing magic if she wanted to live here. I mean, Miss Switzer had already had red soda pop in her pipes, a ten-foot daisy tree next door, and she'd heard that Brownie, who never, ever strayed from his house, had been found at Mrs. Mullins's. There'd been a couple of other minor mishaps that we thought we'd covered up so no one noticed, but we couldn't be sure. Anyway, there was no doubt that even if Miss Switzer didn't know now, she would if we kept doing mixed-up magic. And if Miss Switzer knew, so would the entire town.

It seemed to be a terrible problem. I thought about it so much that my head actually hurt, but there was only one answer I could think of to make everything right — find Mrs. Mullins's recipe book. If she could control the spells, then she could do magic, and no one would ever be the wiser. That all made good sense except for the fact that we'd looked and looked for the magic book, and it was absolutely nowhere to be found.

I just didn't see a way to solve the problem, though I sat on my bed and thought about it almost every night. One night, I picked up the evening newspaper, deciding that it would even be better to do homework than to think about Mrs. Mullins having to leave town.

Miss Jenkins had assigned us to read three newspaper articles for social studies, and I began to look through the paper for the shortest three I could find. Suddenly I saw an advertisement that read: *Auction: Lemmings Moving Company will hold an auction of all unclaimed items at 2:00 P.M., Saturday, April 16.*

Lemmings! I thought to myself. That was the

company that had moved Mrs. Mullins. What if her book is at that auction! The ad gave a phone number, and I copied it down in my notebook. I knew no one would answer at night, but I sure meant to call it the next day. It was probably a real long shot, but at least it was something, and it was certainly better than telling Mrs. Mullins there was no hope at all.

All the way to Mrs. Mullins's house that next afternoon, I tried to decide just how I should tell her about the auction. Would it be worth it to build up her hopes now if we didn't find the recipe book later? I just didn't know.

I finally decided that the best thing was to call the auction place and see what they had to say. I got to Mrs. Mullins's house and went in the other room to call. I tried to make my voice sound low and important, but I was nervous, and I was sure I sounded like a little kid. "Uh, I'd like some information about the auction on Saturday."

"Yes?" replied a lady's voice at the other end of the phone. "What did you want to know?"

What I wanted to know was whether there was a brown recipe book that belonged to Mrs. Mullins being auctioned off, but I didn't think I should come right out and ask that. "Well, uh, could you tell me the way that the auction works?" I asked.

"We're selling items that people left or never claimed when our company moved them. The big items like furniture, refrigerators, and so forth are listed on a sheet of paper which I could send you. The smaller items are put in boxes, and the buyer has to make a bid on the whole box."

"Well, uh, what kind of an item is a recipe book?" I asked hopefully.

"Oh, that would be in a box. It's too small to be considered on its own."

I tried to keep the excitement out of my voice. "Is there a recipe book in any of the boxes?"

"Well, we only have partial records of what we put in the boxes, but let me see. Hmmm, in box seventeen, a recipe book is listed."

"It is? Is it brown? Does it say 'Recipes' on the front?"

"I'm sorry, but I have no idea. The boxes are all sealed. You'll have to come Saturday and bid on the box if you want to open it."

I ran back into the living room. I just had a feeling that Mrs. Mullins's recipe book for magic was waiting patiently for us in box seventeen. I had planned to be real cool about all this, but I saw Mrs. Mullins sitting in a chair looking sadly out the window at the daisy tree, and I just sort of blurted out, "Guess what! Something wonderful might happen on Saturday!"

9

It had taken me awhile to explain everything to
Mrs. Mullins. I'd started at the very beginning
about the way I'd seen the ad and then told her
step by step what I'd done from there.

"Well, Allan" — her face looked brighter than
I'd seen it in days — "I've got to give you credit.
You're a good thinker and a good reader, and
though I don't really think I'll find my book, this
auction certainly merits a try. I'll definitely take
the bus there on Saturday." She began fishing
through her purse, looking for her bus schedule.

"You mean *we'll* go there on Saturday. I want
to be there when you find that book!"

Mrs. Mullins looked pleased that I wanted to
come, but to be perfectly honest, I wasn't doing
it just to keep her company. I had gotten pretty
anxious to get that book back myself, and I knew
that I'd be bursting with curiosity if she were at
the auction and I were at home.

My mom hadn't understood why I'd wanted to

give up my whole Saturday to go to a moving company auction, but she didn't argue about it. Her boss had called a special seminar for everyone in their company on that Saturday, and I think she was relieved that I wouldn't be home all alone. "I'll make it up to you," she promised me. "Next Saturday, you and I will go see a movie." Mom hugged me. "It's been so long since we've had a day just for you and me. You've been such a good kid, and I know it hasn't been easy since Dad and I . . ." She didn't finish the sentence. "Honey, I want you to be happy. Is everything okay at school? Are you still happy at Mrs. Mullins's?"

"Yeah, I guess school is okay. I'd like it more if I could play baseball better, but everything is great with Mrs. Mullins."

"Oh, Allan, I'm sure you're a better baseball player than you think, and I'm so glad you ended up liking Mrs. Mullins so much. I think it's really sweet of you to go with her to that auction thing she wants to attend on Saturday."

Actually I was looking forward to this Saturday as much as Mrs. Mullins, all except for the bus ride, which was going to be long and hot. I'd tried to see if there was a way around it. "Mrs. Mullins," I'd hinted one day while I was in her kitchen, "don't witches have better ways to travel than buses?"

"What do you mean?"

92

I figured a picture was worth a thousand words, so I walked over to the utility closet and got out a broom. Mrs. Mullins began to giggle. "Oh, Allan, you don't really . . ." Then she clapped her hand over her mouth. "Good lordy, you do! Allan, don't you know anything about witches? Why I wouldn't be caught dead on some flimsy broom handle. Obviously the person who started that silly rumor knew nothing at all about witches."

So on Saturday we packed sack lunches and got on the bus. My stomach was so nervous that I was sure I wouldn't be able to eat a thing. Mrs. Mullins looked nervous, too, but she said, "Now, Allan, I'm sure this will be an interesting outing. I've never been to an auction before, but I don't honestly think they've got my recipe book."

I paid no attention to her. They had it. I knew it. She was just afraid to get her hopes up. The bus ride did take practically forever, and we didn't get to the auction until after it had started. Lots of people were sitting in chairs, and a man in the front was pointing to a sofa, a table, or a stove, and then yelling, "WhatamIbidwhatamIbid?"

The people in the chairs who wanted to buy the item were supposed to raise their hands and call out the amount of money that they would pay. I watched two ladies bid back and forth on the ugliest pink sofa I'd ever seen. For a while the auction was very interesting, but it seemed to be taking so much time that I was afraid it would be night before they even started on the boxes.

Finally I heard the man in the front call out, "Box one," and pretty soon, he was up to box ten. He wiped his head with a big red handkerchief. I guess he was getting pretty tired.

"Again, let me remind you that as I call off the box number, I'll read off several items that are in the box. The box may or may not contain other little items that are not listed."

"Remember," I whispered, "we've got to bid on box seventeen!"

"I'm remembering!" said Mrs. Mullins, and I could see that her hand was shaking.

"Box sixteen, three pairs of ladies shoes, four scrapbooks, two scarves, plus more. What am I bid?"

I didn't even hear what he was bid, because his voice boomed out, "Box seventeen, a broken table saw, a man's coat, a recipe book, plus more. What am I bid?"

Mrs. Mullins bid two dollars, but the man behind her bid four. "Raise your bid! Raise your bid!" I called anxiously to her.

"Oh, dear, young man, yoo hoo." Mrs. Mullins voice sounded quite unlike her own. "I'll bid six dollars."

"Sold, to the lady in the red tennis shoes!"

"We did it! We did it!" I reached over and

hugged Mrs. Mullins. We went to the table to pay for the box. The man there warned us that box seventeen was very heavy and asked if we didn't have someone to help us carry it.

"Oh, we'll just open it here," I blurted out. "We only want one thing out of it, and believe me, we can carry that."

The man patted my head. "Okay, sonny! Ma'am, you want me to open it for you?"

"If you would . . . ."

He pried open the lid, and I felt as if my heart were going to jump right out of me. There it was! Right on top was a book clearly marked *Recipes*. Only the book wasn't brown, and the letters weren't gold, and the recipe book definitely wasn't Mrs. Mullins's magic book. It was a book about making hamburgers a hundred ways.

Mrs. Mullins sat down in a chair in the back of the room and put her head in her hands. "Allan, I'm afraid I'm feeling a little weak. I don't think I can go home just now."

I hadn't felt this awful since the day after my dad had moved out of our house. There was nothing I could say then, and there was nothing I could say now.

I walked back over to the box we'd bought, hoping that somehow there was another recipe book in it. I found there was a lot of other junk in it, but no other recipe book. The man who had bid against us walked up to me. "Are you all right, kid? You look a little green."

I wasn't all right, but there was no point in telling the man that. "You can have this box if you want," I said. "It didn't have what we needed."

"Really? Hey, thanks, kid! I fix broken tools, and this old table saw will be a fine project. I bought four other boxes, but I only want the tools out of 'em. Tell you what: I'll open 'em here, and you and your granny can take anything except the tools. It'll be like a trade."

"That's okay, you just take the saw." I knew Mrs. Mullins wouldn't care, and I was too upset to even think about plowing through his boxes. Besides, no one had the only thing we'd really come for. How dumb I had been to think that everything was going to turn out happily-ever-after today.

"No, sonny. We got to trade. Never let it be said that Joshua Andrew Katlin takes somethin' for nothin'."

It was too much trouble to argue. I walked over to his boxes and glanced at them. I'd just take whatever was on top. That way he'd leave me alone. I reached down into the first of his boxes when something in the second caught my eye. "Oh, wow!" I thought I shouted, but actually, I barely whispered. I reached out and touched the brown book almost as if I were afraid it would disappear as soon as my fingers felt it. I ran my hand across the top of the book and traced the gold letters *R-E-C-I-P-E-S*. I don't think I ever said thanks or anything to Mr. Joshua Andrew Katlin. I just hugged the book close to my chest and ran for Mrs. Mullins.

Reaching her chair, I opened my mouth to tell her the good news, but I was in such shock that nothing came out. Mrs. Mullins still had her head buried in her hands, so I tugged at one arm, and put the book on her lap. She felt the weight of it, and her eyes glanced downward. "Oh, lordy, be. Am I dreaming? My book. My magic book." Tears began to roll down her cheeks.

"That's it! That's really it!" I almost did a little dance around Mrs. Mullins. "I can't believe it!"

Mrs. Mullins just sat in her chair staring at the magic book. "I guess I wasn't honestly sure I'd ever see it again."

"Well, we've got it. Oh, Mrs. Mullins, open it!" I could hardly wait to see all those spells. Mrs. Mullins still sat staring at the cover of her book. "Hey, maybe there's a spell we can use so we don't have to take the bus home, and maybe you can do a spell on my arm to help me hit home runs, and maybe we could try a spell to make Miss

Switzer just plain disappear . . . ." I didn't even know exactly what I was saying. I was just so excited that I kept talking.

Mrs. Mullins finally reached over and opened her book. I leaned over her so I could see better. I didn't want to miss one single thing! I meant to find out about every single spell.

"Uh, oh," I said aloud as she turned the first page. "Well, it'll probably get better. I mean, we don't need to know every single spell anyway." But by the time we'd finished looking through the whole book, I couldn't keep the tears out of my eyes. I was suddenly so tired that I just had to sit down. I plopped down on the floor. "If that doesn't beat all," I said glumly. "How could someone have spilled something on all the pages? You can't read one whole spell without part of it being smudged, smeared, or blacked out by that awful spilled stuff." I didn't even care that a tear splashed down my cheek. "I just don't understand it. We tried so hard, we went through so much, and what did we get for all of it? Nothing. Absolutely nothing!"

Mrs. Mullins, stood up as tall as she could, smoothed her skirt, and pushed her glasses up on her nose. "Allan Hobart, how can you say we've got nothing! We've accomplished a lot. For one thing I got my magic book back, and I know it can't fall into the wrong hands. For another, we may not have all of any spell, but at least we can read parts of most of the spells. Isn't that a whole lot more than we ever had before today?" She held her book tightly. "Now, let's stop feeling sorry for ourselves, go home, and see what sense we can make of all of this!"

Mrs. Mullins actually started whistling while we walked back to the bus. As we were riding home, she said, "I think this calls for a celebration. It's too late today, but Monday we'll try a new magic spell."

"But . . . but Miss Switzer is coming back on Sunday. What if she — ?"

Mrs. Mullins interrupted me. "Oh, I'm sure that with my magic book I'll be able to figure out enough of the spells to keep her off guard." Mrs. Mullins bit her lip. "That is, unless her sister tells her about me." She looked at her magic book again. "However, for today, I'm not going to think about that! I'm just going to enjoy holding my recipe book."

I had started our bus trip home feeling grumpy, but by the time we'd gotten all the way there, Mrs. Mullins's good mood had rubbed off on me, and I was getting pretty excited about doing some magic on Monday.

After waiting through a Sunday I thought would never end, Monday finally came. As soon as school was out, I rushed over to Mrs. Mullins's house, threw open the front door, and called, "I'm here! Let's get started with the —"

"Allan," Mrs. Mullins cut me off. "I'm in here with Blanche Switzer."

"Oh . . ." I frowned. I didn't even say hello. What if after everything, Miss Switzer had found out about Mrs. Mullins? The problem with people like Miss Switzer was that they never really listened well enough to understand that some witches were very nice people.

"Miss Switzer was just telling me all about her trip, Allan, and she found out some fascinating information."

Uh, oh, I said to myself, but I kept my face looking as if I didn't care at all.

Miss Switzer totally ignored me. "Anyway, Henrietta, my sister told me all about this witch. She lived in the very next town to Ingleside Inlet. Of course, they got rid of her, but oh, my. They say she once turned her house into a big dungeon and tried to capture all the people. Can you imagine! My sister says her name was Marietta Pullits. We've got to be careful that no one like that moves into this neighborhood! I intend to contact all the realtors in town and tell them to be very careful about selling a house to anyone named Marietta. I mean to keep my eyes open!" She sniffed. "I'll tell you there are a few things around that I don't quite understand, but I'm sure

I will if I keep investigating." Without even pausing for a breath she added, "Well, I've got to be going, Henrietta. I have many people to tell about my trip."

When the door was safely shut behind her, Mrs. Mullins and I looked at each other and laughed. "Marietta Pullits?" I said.

"A dungeon?" She laughed.

"Boy, Miss Switzer sure got mixed-up facts."

"Yes, her facts are a little like our magic."

"Yeah," I said, "but even at its most confused our magic makes more sense and is lots more fun than Blanche Switzer."

Mrs. Mullins green eyes glittered. "Well, I'd have to agree with that. Besides, I'm really beginning to believe that you and I are more than a match for her." Mrs. Mullins took her spell book out of the drawer. "You know, even though I can't read much of my magic book, I sure feel better for having it. Let's go see what we can decipher."

Mrs. Mullins and I walked arm and arm into the kitchen. I opened her magic book and began to read the very few words that were at all legible from the first spell.

"Mrs. Mullins, I don't suppose that your magic book works well enough to use it on my arm?"

"Allan, you don't need magic on your arm. You just need some self-confidence in your heart." I groaned in disgust, but Mrs. Mullins paid no attention. "I'm not kidding, Allan. Jeff said you had a good arm; he even tried to make you a catcher."

"Only once, and he didn't exactly complain when I wouldn't do it." I sighed. "You see, Mrs. Mullins, I can never be sure when my arm's going to be okay, and when my throws are going to be terrible. That's why it's better to stay in the outfield. At least no one cares if I mess up there. Look, let's just talk about your magic book."

10

At school the next day, the guys paired off at recess to play catch. I got my glove out and kind of hung around, but no one asked me to play three-way catch, so I just watched. Then we went to PE. As we walked toward the field, my mouth fell open. I saw Coach talking to a little white-haired lady with red tennis shoes. "Oh, no," I said under my breath.

When we got to the field, Coach met us and blew his whistle. "Okay, listen up! Today, I'm calling the major positions for the teams. Jeff, captain. Steve, captain. Allan, catcher." I didn't even hear the rest of his list. I was mortified. What had Mrs. Mullins told Coach?

"Uh . . . Coach, could I talk to you for a sec?" I asked.

"No time, now. Catch me after the game." He blew his whistle and told us to take our positions. Off behind the backstop, I glimpsed Mrs. Mullins setting up a little chair. I was going to kill her.

My hands were shaking so badly I could barely get my mask and chest protector on. I walked stiffly, and it wasn't just because of the shin guards I had to wear.

Jeff started his warm-up as pitcher. I dropped the first four balls he threw. My fingers felt like big fat salamis. I could see my team glaring at me. "Uh, Coach, I don't feel so well . . . ."

"You can go to the nurse right after the game," he replied unsympathetically. "Let's get this inning started."

The game started, but I didn't. The catcher has to be in on every single play, and I was botching each one. Finally Jeff walked off the mound. "You're not that terrible. I know what you were like when we were playing catch in front of my cousins' house. Geez, Allan, you can do it."

I took a deep breath. I tried to block out everything but the ball. Amazingly that dot of white started landing in my glove, and my throws headed toward the pocket of a teammate's glove. Finally the game was over. Our guys started cheering, and I realized we must have won.

I just stood there. It was only one dumb PE baseball game, but I had never been so tired or happy in my whole life. Then I noticed Steve and Jeff up ahead of me. Steve was talking. "Okay, Jeff, so your team beat us today. I'm still ahead for the year. You just lucked out getting Hobart.

Who'd have ever thought he could catch?"

The guys were all heading in to the classroom, but I had to know. I glanced around to make certain no one was watching, and then I ran to the fence. Behind it, Henrietta Mullins was quietly folding up her little chair. She glanced up at me. "Nice game."

"Mrs. Mullins," I whispered urgently, "did you use magic to make my arm work right?"

"Sorry, Allan, baseball magic is out of my department. I just told the coach I was an old family friend who had come especially to see you play catcher, and could he please arrange it. Beyond that, I guess you must have made your own magic."

"But . . ."

Mrs. Mullins' green eyes sparkled, and the corners of her mouth tugged at a smile. "Oh, yes, I'd almost forgotten. Weren't you the fourth-grader who told me you didn't believe in witches and magic and all that sort of thing?"

"Mrs. Mullins . . ." I started to say, but the baby-sitter I had thought I didn't need, the witch whose magic created marvelous, mixed-up fun, and the best friend I ever could have wished for, had already turned and begun walking home.